AMERICAN HISTORY, CULTURE AND LITERATURE

THE CHICAGO MASSACRE OF 1812

AMERICAN HISTORY, CULTURE AND LITERATURE

Additional books and e-books in this series can be found on Nova's website under the Series tab.

AMERICAN HISTORY, CULTURE AND LITERATURE

THE CHICAGO MASSACRE OF 1812

JOSEPH KIRKLAND

Copyright © 2019 by Nova Science Publishers, Inc.

All rights reserved. No part of this book may be reproduced, stored in a retrieval system or transmitted in any form or by any means: electronic, electrostatic, magnetic, tape, mechanical photocopying, recording or otherwise without the written permission of the Publisher.

We have partnered with Copyright Clearance Center to make it easy for you to obtain permissions to reuse content from this publication. Simply navigate to this publication's page on Nova's website and locate the "Get Permission" button below the title description. This button is linked directly to the title's permission page on copyright.com. Alternatively, you can visit copyright.com and search by title, ISBN, or ISSN.

For further questions about using the service on copyright.com, please contact:
Copyright Clearance Center
Phone: +1-(978) 750-8400   Fax: +1-(978) 750-4470   E-mail: info@copyright.com.

NOTICE TO THE READER

The Publisher has taken reasonable care in the preparation of this book, but makes no expressed or implied warranty of any kind and assumes no responsibility for any errors or omissions. No liability is assumed for incidental or consequential damages in connection with or arising out of information contained in this book. The Publisher shall not be liable for any special, consequential, or exemplary damages resulting, in whole or in part, from the readers' use of, or reliance upon, this material. Any parts of this book based on government reports are so indicated and copyright is claimed for those parts to the extent applicable to compilations of such works.

Independent verification should be sought for any data, advice or recommendations contained in this book. In addition, no responsibility is assumed by the Publisher for any injury and/or damage to persons or property arising from any methods, products, instructions, ideas or otherwise contained in this publication.

This publication is designed to provide accurate and authoritative information with regard to the subject matter covered herein. It is sold with the clear understanding that the Publisher is not engaged in rendering legal or any other professional services. If legal or any other expert assistance is required, the services of a competent person should be sought. FROM A DECLARATION OF PARTICIPANTS JOINTLY ADOPTED BY A COMMITTEE OF THE AMERICAN BAR ASSOCIATION AND A COMMITTEE OF PUBLISHERS.

Additional color graphics may be available in the e-book version of this book.

Library of Congress Cataloging-in-Publication Data

ISBN: 978-1-53616-197-7

Published by Nova Science Publishers, Inc. † New York

Contents

List of Illustrations		vii
Preface		xi
Part I.	Saturday, August Fifteenth, 1812, Narratives of the Massacre	1
Part II.	Historical and Biographical How Chicago Began and Who Were Its Beginners	33
Chapter 1	The Dark Before the Dawn	35
Chapter 2	Building of the First Fort Dearborn	47
Chapter 3	English and Indian Savages	59
Chapter 4	A Long Farewell	67
Chapter 5	Fate of the Fugitives	79
Chapter 6	John Kinzie's Captivity	89
Chapter 7	Contemporaneous Reports	95
Appendix A.		113
Appendix B.		123
Appendix C.		135
Appendix D.		143

Appendix E.	**165**
Appendix F.	**179**
Appendix G.	**193**
Appendix H.	**199**
Appendix I.	**203**
Appendix K.	**207**
Index	**215**
Related Nova Publications	**221**

LIST OF ILLUSTRATIONS

Figure 1.	Early Jesuit.		35
Figure 2.	Little Turtle—Me-Che-Kan-Nah-Quah.		37
Figure 3.	General Anthony Wayne. From "Cyclopædia of United States History."—Copyright 1881, by Harper & Brothers.		39
Figure 4.	William Whistler.		40
Figure 5.	Mrs. William Whistler. From a photograph taken during her visit to Chicago in 1875.		42
Figure 6.	Charles Jouett.		44
Figure 7.	A "red-coat" of 1812.		47
Figure 8.	Fort Dearborn, 1803-4. (Fergus' Series, No. 16)		49
Figure 9.	Cabin in the Woods.		53
Figure 10.	Kinzie Mansion—1812.		55
Figure 11.	Human Scalp.		57
Figure 12.	Indian Warrior.		59
Figure 13.	George Third.		66
Figure 14.	Squaw.		69

Figure 15.	Black Partridge Medal. From "Cyclopædia of United States History."Copyright, 1881, by Harper & Brothers.	73
Figure 16.	William Wells.	75
Figure 17.	Rebekah (Wells) Heald.	76
Figure 18.	Alexander Robinson (in old age). Chief of the Pottowatomies, Chippewas, and others.	83
Figure 19.	Tecumseh. From "Cyclopædia of United States History."—Copyright, 1881, by Harper & Brothers.	88
Figure 20.	New Fort, River, Kinzie House, Etc., as Given in Wau-Bun.	93
Figure 21.	Massacre Tree, 18th Street.	95
Figure 22.	The Second Block-House in Its Last Days.	102
Figure 23.	Block-House Tablet.	107
Figure 24.	Beaubien Fiddle and Calumet, In Possession of the Calumet Club.	108
Figure 25.	Cock-Crow.	113
Figure 26.	Robert Cavelier, Sieur De La Salle.	114
Figure 27.	George Rogers Clark (Late in Life). From "Cyclopædia of United States History." —Copyright 1881, by Harper & Brothers.	115
Figure 28.	Shaubena in Old Age. (About 1856.)	119
Figure 29.	Chicago River. Junction of North and South Branches (1830).	122
Figure 30.	Interior of New Fort (1850), Lake House in the Distance.	128
Figure 31.	Waubansa Stone with Great Fire Relics.	129

List of Illustrations

Figure 32.	Wild Onion.	**134**
Figure 33.	Mrs. Gwenthlean [Whistler] Kinzie (1891).	**137**
Figure 34.	John K. Clark.	**146**
Figure 35.	Archibald Clybourn.	**147**
Figure 36.	Mrs. Juliette Kinzie (1856). Author of "Wau-Bun."	**151**
Figure 37.	John Harris Kinzie (1827). From a miniature in possession of the Kinzie family.	**152**
Figure 38.	John Harris Kinzie in Later Life.	**155**
Figure 39.	Robert Allen Kinzie.	**156**
Figure 40.	Kinzie Mansion as Given in Wau-Bun.	**158**
Figure 41.	Gurdon Saltonstall Hubbard, in Middle Life.	**159**
Figure 42.	Mrs. Nellie (Kinzie) Gordon.	**161**
Figure 43.	John Harris Kinzie, Jr.	**162**
Figure 44.	Darius Heald, with Sword and Other Massacre Relics.	**172**
Figure 45.	Massacre Tree and Part of Pullman House.	**178**
Figure 46.	Remains unearthed April 26th and presented to the Historical Society July 27, 1891.	**180**
Figure 47.	Gurdon Saltonstall Hubbard. (Last picture taken of him.)	**183**
Figure 48.	The Late Calumet Club-House.	**192**
Figure 49.	The Sauganash (1833).	**196**
Figure 50.	Me-Tee-A; A Signer of the Treaty of 1821.	**200**
Figure 51.	Farewell War-Dance of the Indians, August 18, 1835.	**204**

PREFACE*

History is not a snap-shot. Events happen, and the true record of them follows at a distance. Sometimes the early report is too voluminous, and it takes time to reduce it to truth by a winnowing process that divides chaff from grain. This has been the case regarding every great modern battle. Sometimes, on the other hand, the event was obscure and became important through the rise of other, later conditions; in which case, instead of winnowing, the historian sets himself to gleaning the field and making his grist out of scattered bits of its fruitage. This has been the case regarding the Chicago massacre of 1812.

It was only a skirmish and a slaughter, involving the loss of three-score lives. But those dead men, women and children were the fore-runners of all the dwellers in one of the greatest cities of Christendom, the renowned city of Chicago.

Up to less than twenty years ago it was thought—by the few who gave the matter any thought—that next to nothing could ever be found out concerning the events which took place in and about Fort Dearborn—now Chicago—on August 15, 1812, and the time immediately before and after that day. All that was then known was contained in the artless, non-historic

---

* This is an edited, augmented and reformatted version of "The Chicago Massacre of 1812" by Joseph Kirkland, originally published by The Dribble Publishing Company, dated 1893. The views, opinions, and nomenclature expressed in this book are those of the authors and do not reflect the views of Nova Science Publishers, Inc.

narrative contained in Mrs. Kinzie's amusing and delightful story of her own adventures (1831-1833), into which she wove, as a mere episode, the scattered reminiscences of members of her family who had taken part in the tragedy of twenty years before.

But in 1881, ten years after the Great Fire had wiped out all old Chicago, and all records of older Chicago, the Historical Society happily took up the task of erecting a "massacre memorial tablet" on the ground where Fort Dearborn had stood. William M. Hoyt generously gave the necessary money, and the Hon. John Wentworth ably and devotedly set himself about gathering, from all over the land, every item which could be gleaned to throw light on the dark and dreadful event. How well he succeeded is shown by his book, "Fort Dearborn," published by the Fergus Printing Company as number 16 in its admirable Historical Series; a collection of pamphlets which should form part of every library in the city.

Exhaustive as was Mr. Wentworth's research, yet the last word had not been said. There was—and is—still living, the Hon. Darius Heald, son of the Captain (Nathan) Heald who commanded the whites on the fatal day, and who, with his wife, was sorely wounded in the fray. The son had heard, a hundred times, his parents' story of the massacre; and his repetition of that story taken down in short-hand from his own lips, forms the main part of the strictly new matter I offer in this book.

Much of the contents of the following pages, which has been published before, is not marked as quotation, for the reason that it is my own writing, having been included in my "Story of Chicago," published by the same house which publishes this book. (Many of the illustrations are also taken from this same source.) On the other hand, much that is marked in quotation is also my own work; but as it is part of my contribution to Munsell & Company's large "History of Chicago" which is still in press, credit is invariably given to the last-named work.

All I could find, on this fascinating theme, I have faithfully recorded. If a later gleaner shall find more, no one will be more glad than will I, to welcome it.

Joseph Kirkland.

Part I. Saturday, August Fifteenth, 1812, Narratives of the Massacre

The morning of Fort Dearborn's fatal day dawned bright and clear over Lake Michigan and the sandy flat. The "reveille" doubtless was sounded before sun-rise; and one can imagine the rattle of the drum and scream of the fife as they broke the dewy stillness and floated away, over the sand-spit and out on the lake; across the river to the Kinzie house and its outbuilding, the Ouillemette house; and up stream to the Indian encampments, large, dark and lowering. Quite possibly the tune then prescribed was the same as that now used for the drum-fife reveille, together with the words that have attached themselves to it of late years:

> Wake ye lazy soldiers, rouse up and be killed, Hard tack and salt horse, get your gizzard filled. Then go to fighting—fire your forty round— Fall dead and lay there buried under ground.

If this time-honored (and much hated) tune has come down to us from so long, the words had on that morning a significance even more perfect than that ordinarily belonging to them.

Early the company cooks must have been at work, boiling whole barrels of salt pork which had been in soak for days beforehand, and as much fresh beef as could possibly be used before spoiling. Bread had doubtless been baked and packed earlier in the week, and now all imaginable preparations for a march of nearly a month must be completed and the utensils packed and loaded into the company wagons. At each of the other, smaller households outside the fort similar toils and cares were going on. How were the lately weaned little ones to be cared for? Perhaps some parents hoped that they could drive their milch-cows with the caravan, seeing that grass was plenty and progress would be necessarily slow. What did the prospective mothers hope and fear? The wife of Phelim Corbin; how did she arm her soul for the month of rough travel, with the travail of child birth as one of its terrors?

Certainly the happiest of the crowd were the unconscious little ones, sure of love and care, full of hope and curiosity—a round dozen of them in one wagon, beginning the first journey of their innocent lives—the first and last. Fancy the mothers tucking them in! The eager little faces upturned for good-bye kisses!

All the workers might have spared themselves their trouble. If they were thinking of their cows, the crack of the Indian rifles soon ended that care. The food was enough and to spare; not a morsel of it did they ever eat. The journey of a month dwindled to a tramp of an hour; and as to the precious children—

Captain William Wells had come, with thirty friendly Indians (Miamis) to guard and help them through their long, lonely tramp to Detroit. He was a white man, the uncle of the commandant's young wife (Rebekah Wells Heald), but had been stolen when a boy by the Indians and brought up by them; had married a chief's daughter and had fought on their side until, years ago, this same young niece had gone to him and persuaded him to come back to his own kith and kin. So any fears the helpless settlers might have felt at first could now surely be put aside—Wells was so strong, so brave, so well acquainted with the Indians! He could doubtless keep them in order, either by policy or by force.

But if all was well, why had Captain Wells blackened his face—that is, put on the Indian sign of war and death—before starting that morning? All accounts agree that he did so, and usually it is taken as having been a sign of consciousness of impending death. Mrs. Helm[1] seems to have regarded it in this light. The question can never be settled, but to me it seems to have been an act of policy; an effort to identify himself with his Miamis and other friendly Indians. Wau-Bun adds the gruesome and almost incredible story that the start out was made to the music of the dead march! As Mrs. Helm was on horseback with the column she must have known, and we can but take her word for it.

The large herd of beef-cattle was left to the savages. This was probably the most precious gift of all put in their hands by the abandonment of the post. The liquor, if it had been left, would have been their bane, and the fire-arms the mere instruments of mutual destruction. The clothes must

---

[1] Margaret Helm, wife of Lieutenant Helm, and step-daughter of old John Kinzie, has hitherto been the main—almost the only—source of knowledge about the massacre. She told the story twenty years after its occurrence, to Mrs. John H. Kinzie, who embodied it in her romantic narrative "Wau-Bun," published about twenty-two years later still.

wear out, the flour be eaten up, the tools and furniture useless, the paints and gew-gaws a fleeting joy; but the herd! This would be self-sustaining, self-perpetuating, a perennial fount of blessing and mine of wealth. Here were food, clothing, shoes for this year and all years to come. No tribe or nation of their race had ever possessed such a treasure. How did they avail themselves of it? Wau-Bun answers:

> The fort had become a scene of plunder to such as remained after the troops moved out. The cattle had been shot down as they ran at large and lay dead or dying around. This work of butchery had commenced just as we were leaving the fort.

No more characteristic bit of Indian painting has ever been made than that given in these few words. Here was the native savage (not ignorant of wiser ways, for he had had the thrifty white man under his eyes for four generations) still showing himself in sense a child, in strength a man, and in cruelty a fiend incarnate.

Mrs. Helm continues:

> I well remember a remark of Ensign Ronan, as the firing went on. "Such," turning to me, "is to be our fate—to be shot down like beasts."
>
> "Well, sir," said the commanding officer, who overheard him, "are you afraid?"
>
> "No," replied the high-spirited young man, "I can march up to the enemy where you dare not show your face!" And his subsequent gallant behavior showed this to be no idle boast.

Unconsciously Mrs. Helm, in this artless tale told to glorify the younger officer, awakens in our minds a feeling of dislike for him. That a youth, scarce two years out of West Point, should add an ill-timed insult to the heavy cares of his senior officer, a soldier of thirteen years service, must be shocking to everyone. Seeing that within two hours he was to die in action, bravely doing his duty (in company with his senior similarly engaged and sorely wounded) we can readily forgive his error, but not without a protest against a foolish woman's foolish effort to make it out a noble and praiseworthy outburst.

Mrs. Heald's narrative[2] (though fortified by Captain Heald's letter, quoted later) seems less probable than the foregoing circumstantial account in Wau-Bun. She says:

> The fort was vacated quietly, not a cross word being passed between soldiers and Indians, and good-byes were exchanged. Not an officer objected to leaving. Nobody objected but Kinzie, who did so for personal reasons. Everything left was divided among the Indians who were there, and a party of them escorted the whites out of the fort, these Indians being the ones who took no interest in the fight, although they may have known something about it. The general impression among the officers (and this was Captain Heald's idea also) was that the Indians who took their share when the things were distributed at the fort, had no part in the massacre.

Captain Heald's force consisted of fifty-four regular soldiers and twelve militia-men, and with them departed every white inhabitant of the little settlement, men, women and children—probably about thirty in all—ranging in social condition from the prosperous Kinzies to the humble discharged soldiers who had married and started to make a living by tilling the soil, etc.

The Kinzie family was to go by boat, skirting along the lake and keeping in touch with the land column as long as it should hug the shore; later ascending the St. Joseph's River to "Bertrand," or "Parc-aux-vaches," as it was called, in memory of its having been the cow-pasture of the old French-Canadian settlement and fort which had stood on the bank of that river a century or so ago. The boat-party consisted of Mrs. John Kinzie, her son, John H., born at Sandwich, Canada, July 7, 1803, and her other children—Ellen Marion (later Mrs. Alexander Wolcott), born in Chicago,

---

[2] It is a curious fact that all our direct information concerning the events of that day comes from two women. Mrs. Lieutenant Helm, who has been already mentioned, and Mrs. Captain Heald. Both these young wives will receive more detailed mention a little further on. Mrs. Heald's account has never been published before. I give it as taken down in short-hand from the lips of her son, the Hon. Darius Heald of O'Fallon, Missouri, in the summer of 1892.

December, 1805; Maria Indiana (later Mrs. General Hunter), born in Chicago, in 1807, and Robert A., born in Chicago in 1810. Her daughter by a previous marriage, Margaret McKillip, was, it will be remembered, now the wife of Lieutenant Helm, and she bravely elected to share the perils of the land-march with her husband. There was also in the boat the nurse, Josette (misprinted in Wau-Bun, "Grutte")[3] Laframboise (afterward Mrs. Jean Baptiste Beaubien), a clerk of Mr. Kinzie's, two servants, the boatman, and two Indians as guard. This shows that the boat must have been neither a bark canoe nor a common "dug-out" or "pirogue," but a large bateau, capable of carrying these numerous passengers, with corresponding baggage and supplies.

Grutti

To-pee-nee-be, a friendly Indian, chief of the St. Joseph's band, early in the morning of the fatal day, had warned John Kinzie that trouble was to come from the "escort" which Captain Heald had bargained for with the Pottowatomies in council, and had urged him to go in the boat with his family. But the old frontiers-man was built of too sturdy stuff to take such advice. If there was to be danger he must share it, and if help would avail he must give it; so he rode with the column.

First rode out Captain William Wells, hero-martyr, marching, probably consciously, to a doom self-inflicted under the impulse of human sympathy and soldierly honor. Following him were half of his mounted escort of Miami Indians, followed in their turn by the volunteers and such of the regulars as were able to bear arms. Next came the short train of wagons, with stores, supplies, camp-equippage, women, children, sick, wounded and disabled. This little caravan contained all there was to show for eight

---

[3] In the Story of Chicago is given the following fac simile to show how readily the name "Josette" might have been read "Grutte."

years of industry and privation. But what mattered it? Greater savings would only have meant greater loss, and more men, women and children would only have meant more suffering and death.

The rear-guard was composed of the remainder of Captain Wells's wretched Miamis, such reliance as is a broken reed. The Miamis were mounted, as were Captain Wells, Mr. Kinzie, Mrs. Heald and Mrs. Helm, but probably no others of the party.

The day continued bright and sunny, and the line must have stretched from the fort (about the south end of Rush Street bridge) perhaps to the present Madison Street, half way to the point where began the sand-dunes or low hills which, even within the memory of the present generation, skirted the shores down as far as the beginning of the oak woods of Hyde Park. The bateau followed in the rear of the column and had just reached the mouth of the river (where the foot of Madison street now is[4]) when a messenger from To-pe-nee-be brought the Kinzie party to a halt.

The column had marched parallel with the Pottowatomie "escort" until both bodies reached the sand-hills. Then the whites kept by the shore-road, while the Indians, veering slightly to their right, put the sand-hills between their crowd and the slim, weak line of troops and wagons.

The reports of the fight itself, given by the two witnesses on whom we must rely, do not differ materially from each other. Mrs. Helm's narrative naturally treats more fully of the Kinzie family's experiences; Mrs. Heald's more fully of her own adventures and the death of her uncle. Neither woman mentions the other; they were probably separated early. I will give the stories in turn, beginning with Mrs. Helm's.

MARGARET HELM'S STORY

The boat started, but had scarcely reached the mouth of the river, which, it will be recollected, was here half a mile below the fort, when another messenger from To-pe-nee-be arrived to detain them where they

---

[4] The river then made a turn southward just east of the fort, and only found an entrance to the lake across the south end of a long sand-bar, the continuation of the shore of the North Side.

were. In breathless expectation sat the wife and mother. She was a woman of uncommon energy and strength of character, yet her heart died within her as she folded her arms around her helpless infants and gazed on the march of her husband and her eldest child [Mrs. Helm] to certain destruction.

They had marched perhaps a mile and a half [Fourteenth Street], when Captain Wells, who had kept somewhat in advance of his Miamis, came riding furiously back. "They are about to attack us!" he shouted. "Form instantly and charge upon them." Scarcely were the words uttered when a volley was showered from among the sand-hills. The troops were hastily brought into line and charged up the bank. One man, a veteran of seventy winters, fell as they ascended.

After we had left the bank the firing became general. The Miamis fled at the outset. Their chief rode up to the Pottowatomies and said: "You have deceived the Americans and us. You have done a bad action, and (brandishing his tomahawk) I will be the first to head a party of Americans to return and punish your treachery." So saying he galloped after his companions, who were now scouring across the prairies.

Mrs. Helm does not say that she heard these words when uttered, nor is it probable that she could have been within hearing distance of the very head of the column, or even could have understood the words unless (what most unlikely) they were uttered in English. The whole circumstance looks apocryphal—probably a later Indian fabrication.

> The troops behaved most gallantly. They were but a handful, but they seemed resolved to sell their lives as dearly as possible. Our horses pranced and bounded and could hardly be restrained as the balls whistled among them. I drew off a little and gazed upon my husband and father, who were yet unharmed, I felt that my hour was come, and endeavored to forget those I loved and prepare myself for my approaching fate.

This seems to be the moment where her narrative diverges from that of Mrs. Heald, who evidently followed the troops, as she was caught between a cross-fire of the Indians, whom the advance had left on its flanks and rear, and there received her wounds. Mrs. Helm's subsequent narrative shows that she was, when rescued, unwounded and near the Like.

> While I was thus engaged, the surgeon, Dr. Van Voorhees, came up. He was badly wounded. His horse was shot under him and he had received a ball in his leg. Every muscle of his face was quivering with the agony of terror. He said to me:
> "Do you think they will take our lives? I am badly wounded, but I think not mortally. Perhaps we might purchase our lives by promising a large reward. Do you think there is any chance?"
> "Dr. VanVoorhees," said I, "do not let us waste the few moments that yet remain to us in such vain hopes. Our fate is inevitable. In a few minutes we must appear before the bar of God. Let us make what preparation is yet in our power."
> "O, I cannot die!" exclaimed he. "I am not fit to die—if I had but a short time to prepare—death is awful!"
> I pointed to Ensign Ronan, who, though mortally wounded and nearly down, was still fighting with desperation on one knee. "Look at that man," said I; "at least he dies like a soldier."
> "Yes," replied the unfortunate man, with a gasp, "but he has no terrors of the future. He is an unbeliever."

When we read this remarkable dialogue—remarkable as occurring amid the rattle of musketry on a battle-field where the narrators' friends were perishing in a hopeless struggle with an overpowering force of savage foes—we remember that Mrs. Kinzie's book did not assume to be history; was not written as a grave and literal record of things as they were; a statement carefully scrutinized to see that no unjust slur is cast upon any character, even so unimportant a one as the poor wounded, dying surgeon. Mrs. Helm, on the dreadful day, was a mere girl-wife of seventeen years, and was a woman of thirty-seven when Mrs. Kinzie transcribed the artless tale into Wau-Bun, a book which reads like a romance, and was meant so to be read.

The utterance of these admirable sentiments while still in sight of Ensign Ronan, mortally wounded, yet fighting with desperation on one knee, again puts us in doubt as to Mrs. Helm's location on the field; but the next part of her story shows that she was not far from the water.

At this moment a young Indian raised his tomahawk at me. By springing aside I avoided the blow, which was intended for my skull, but which alighted on my shoulder. I seized him around the neck, and while exerting my utmost efforts to get possession of his scalping-knife, which hung in a scabbard over his breast, I was dragged from his grasp by another and an older Indian. The latter bore me struggling and resisting toward the lake. Notwithstanding the rapidity with which I was hurried along, I recognized, as I passed them, the remains of the unfortunate surgeon. Some murderous tomahawk had stretched him upon the very spot where I had last seen him.

I was immediately plunged into the water and held there with a forcible hand, notwithstanding my resistance. I soon perceived, however, that the object of my captor was not to drown me, for he held me firmly in such a position as to place my head above water. This reassured me, and regarding him attentively I soon recognized, in spite of the paint with which he was disguised, *The Black Partridge.*

This picturesque narrative of the rescue of a young bride by a friendly Indian, has been justly regarded as the one romantic story connected with that dark and bloody day. It has been the chosen theme of the story-teller, the painter and the sculptor, and its portrayal in perennial bronze forms the theme of the magnificent group which has been designed and modeled by the sculptor, Carl Rohl-Smith, cast in bronze, and presented (June, 1893), with appropriate ceremonies, to the Chicago Historical Society, "in trust for the city and for posterity" as set forth by an inscription on its granite base.[5]

Mrs. Helm goes on:

> When the firing had nearly subsided my preserver bore me from the water and conducted me up the sand-banks. It was a burning August morning, and walking through the sand in my drenched condition was inexpressibly painful and fatiguing. I stooped and took off my shoes to free them from the sand with which they were nearly filled, when a squaw seized and bore them off, and I was obliged to proceed without them.
>
> When we had gained the prairie [probably at about Twelfth Street] I was met by my father [her step-father, John Kinzie], who told me that my husband was safe, but slightly wounded. They led me gently back toward the Chicago River, along the southern bank of which was the Pottowatomie encampment. At one time I was placed on a horse without a saddle, but finding the motion insupportable, I sprang off. Supported partly by my kind conductor, Black Partridge, and partly by another Indian, Pee-so-tum, who held dangling in his hand a scalp which, by the black ribbon around the queue, I recognized as that of Captain Wells, I dragged my fainting steps to one of the wigwams. The wife of Wah-bee-nee-mah, a chief from the Illinois River, was standing near, and seeing my exhausted condition, she seized a kettle, dipped up some water from the stream that flowed near [the slough that emptied into the main river at about the south end of State Street bridge], threw into it some maple sugar, and stirring it up with her hand, gave it to me to drink. This act of kindness in the midst of so many horrors touched me most sensibly, but my attention was soon diverted to other objects.
>
> The whites had surrendered after the loss of about two-thirds their number. They had stipulated, through the interpreter, Peresh Leclerc, for the preservation of their lives and those of the remaining women and

---

[5] See Appendix K.

children, and for their delivery at some of the British posts, unless ransomed by traders in the Indian country. It appears that the wounded prisoners were not considered as included in the stipulation, and a horrible scene ensued on their being brought into camp. An old squaw, infuriated by the loss of friends, or excited by the sanguinary scenes around her, seemed possessed by a demoniac ferocity. She seized a stable-fork and assaulted one miserable victim who lay groaning and writhing in the agony of his wounds, aggravated by the scorching beams of the sun. With a delicacy of feeling scarcely to have been expected under such circumstances, Wah-bee-nee-mah stretched a mat across two poles, between me and the deadful scene. I was thus spared, in some degree, a view of its horrors, although I could not entirely close my ears to the cries of the sufferer.

The disgrace attaching to the British government in seeking alliance with such savages in a war against civilized beings of its own race, is elsewhere fully treated. One can only wish that those cries might have reached the women of all England, instead of falling fruitlessly on those of one poor, exhausted, helpless American girl, and of the red hell-spawn grinning and dancing with delight at the sound.

Such is the tale as first given to the world by Mrs. Kinzie in "Wau-Bun." I will now present the narrative of the same struggle, defeat, surrender and massacre as often told by Mrs. Captain Heald to her son, the Hon. Darius Heald, and by him to me. The two are not, in essentials, contradictory; each completes and rounds out the other.

After giving the account of the peaceable start from the fort (inconsistent with Mrs. Helm's story, already quoted, and less truth-seeming than the latter), she goes on to say:

REBEKAH HEALD'S STORY

Captain Wells' escort was mounted on Indian ponies. Captain Wells himself was mounted on a thoroughbred. Mrs. Heald and Mrs. Helm were also on horseback, the former on her own beloved Kentucky horse.

Part I. 13

They advanced, Wells and his escort getting about a quarter of a mile ahead, and were jogging along quietly when all at once they halted, and he turned back and got down pretty close to Captain Heald—perhaps half the distance. He pulled off his hat and swung it around his head once or twice, making a circle. As soon as he saw Wells coming back, Captain Heald said to his wife: "Uncle sees something ahead of him there. There is something wrong." And when he made the circle around his head, Mrs. Heald understood the sign, "We are surrounded by Indians." Captain Wells soon got close enough to shout "We are surrounded by Indians. March up on the sand-ridges. There are sand-ridges we ought to get in behind where we can stand half up and not be seen." Then she saw the Indians' heads "sticking up and down again, here and there, like turtles out of the water." They marched up on the sand-ridges, the wagons being put back next to the lake and the men taking position in front of them. Captain Wells shouted to Captain Heald, "Charge them!" and then led on and broke the ranks of the Indians, who scattered right and left. He then whirled round and charged to the left. This move brought them well out into the country, and they marched onward and took position about two or three hundred yards in front of the wagons and a like distance from the Indians. Captain Heald rather gave way to Captain Wells, knowing his superior excellence in Indian warfare, Wells having been trained from childhood by such warriors as Little Turtle, Tecumseh and Black Hawk; especially by the first two.

Here to the eye of common-sense, whether soldierly or civilian, the battle is already gone—lost beyond salvation. The onus of blame appears to rest on poor Wells, the brave, devoted volunteer. He had learned war in a school that took no account of the supply-train; in the school of individual fighters, living on nothing, saving no wounded or non-combatants; dash, scurry, kill, scalp and run away, every man for himself—and the devil take the hindmost—in other words the Indian system. As to this band of whites, what had it to fight for but its train of wagons with all the helpless ones, all the stores, all the ammunition, all the means of progress and of caring for the wounded? To charge the centre of a brave, unformed rabble which outflanks you is only heroic suicide at best, and when the doing so leaves the train at the mercy of the spreading flanks of the foe, it is fatal madness.

To return to the Heald narrative:

> Another charge was made which enabled Captain Wells to get a little closer to the Indians. He had two pistols and a small gun. His bullets and powder were kept in shoulder belts, hung at convenient places, and he generally had an extra bullet in his mouth, which helped him to load fast when necessary. He could pour in a little powder, wad it down, "blow in" the bullet, prime and fire more quickly than one can tell the facts. The Indians broke from him right and left. The hottest part of the battle lasted but a few minutes, but Captain Heald's little band was cut down. He gave the signal for surrender; the chiefs came together and they made a compromise.

By this time Wells, Ronan and Van Vorhees were killed, Heald had a bullet in his hip, Mrs. Heald had a half dozen wounds, half the regulars were killed or wounded, and so far as we now know for certain, all twelve militia-men. (A doubt about this last named unexplained mortality, and suggestion as to the probable manner of their death, will be noted later.) Darius Heald could only say:

> Afterwards, in talking the matter over, Captain Nathan Heald said that he had no confidence in the Indians, but that he had done the best he could do; that in fifteen minutes more the last man would have been killed, as they had no chance at all; his men were falling rapidly, and he himself was wounded in the hip by a one-ounce ball. That ball was never extracted, and caused his death twenty years afterward.

In any circumstances, one cannot cast blame on a beaten commander, negotiating with his victorious foes, while bleeding from a bullet deep-bedded in his hip-joint. In this case, it is not likely that blame would be due, even if Captain Heald had been unhurt. But for his surrender, the Chicago Massacre would have been, on a small scale, the fore-runner of the great Custer slaughter, where not a white man lived to tell the tale.

Every man, woman and child of white blood (except perhaps the Kinzies and Lieutenant Helm), would now be in oblivion almost as if they had never been born. Even the "massacre tree" that stands to-day (1893) in Eighteenth street near the lake, in gaunt, leafless old age, could only have been identified by the bleaching skulls, great and small, which surrounded it when General Cass passed the spot a few years afterward.

Here we take up again Mrs. Heald's personal story:

> After the fighting commenced, Mrs. Heald turned back and ascended a little elevation between the army and the wagons. She saw a young, fine-looking officer fall [probably Lieutenant Ronan] and thought it was her husband, and was under this impression until after the fight was over. Just before the surrender, she got up in range of the bullets coming from Indians on both sides of her. She did not know whether the Indians aimed at her or not, but she was wounded in six places, one hand being rendered helpless, the ball passing between the two bones of her arm. Her son has seen the scar a thousand times.

I have remarked that Mrs. Heald does not mention the presence of Mrs. Helm, nor does the latter that of the former. We judge from this, and from Mrs. Helm's account of her being saved by being plunged in the lake, that the latter remained nearer the shore than did the other.

DEATH OF CAPTAIN WELLS

> Captain Wells, who was shot through the lungs, rode up and took her hand, saying: "Farewell my child." Mrs. Heald said to him: "Why uncle, I hope you will get over this." "No my child," he said, "lean not." He told her he was shot through the lungs, and she saw the blood oozing through his nose and mouth. He still held her hand and talked to her, saying that he could not last five minutes longer. He said: "Tell my wife—if you live to get there, but I think it doubtful if a single one gets there—tell her I died at my post doing the best I could. There are seven red devils over there that I have killed."

His horse, which had been shot just behind the girth, then fell and caught Captain Wells' leg under him. As he did so, Captain Wells turned and saw six or seven Indians approaching them. He took aim and fired, killing one of them. They approached still closer, and Mrs. Heald said to him: "Uncle, there is an Indian pointing right at the back of your head." Captain Wells put his hand back and held up his head that better aim might be taken, and then cried "Shoot away!" The Indian fired, the shot being fatal. They then pulled him out from under his horse (Mrs. Heald still seated on her horse nearby) and cut his body open, the gashes being in the shape of a cross. They took out his heart, placed it on a gun-stick and whirled it round and round, yelling like fiends. The noise drew other Indians to the spot and they then commenced cutting up the heart and eating it. They crowded around and the bleeding heart was thrust forward at one after another.

Finally an Indian cut off a piece, held it up to Mrs. Heald and insisted on her eating it. She shook her head. He then daubed her face with it. She shook her fist at him. Then they called her "Epeconier! Epeconier!" this being their name for Captain Wells—thus signifying that she was a Wells—a person full of pluck and fortitude.

So nobly perished one of the best and bravest frontiers-men, fighting where he had been summoned by sympathy and affection, not by the orders of any superior officer. No knight ever set lance in rest under a more purely chivalric impulse than did this plain, pretending, half-educated pioneer. Two hundred and fifty miles away he had heard the warning note of peril, seen the fair young face of his brother's daughter (she who long before had sought him out among his savage captors and restored him to his kins-folk), and felt the impulse of manly self-devotion to save her and her friends from impending doom. He obeyed the noble impulse and—he died like a man, and somewhere beneath our thoughtless footsteps his bones lie buried.[6]

---

[6] Chicago should not be without a statue of this early hero, martyred in her service. A miniature exists purporting to give his features, and as to his form, that could be easily reproduced from description, while his Indian dress would serve to give grace and dignity to the work. Among the first streets named, when the village of Chicago was laid out (1831), was one called after him—for he was not yet forgotten. Part of the street-the stretch north of the river—still retains the great name, but the most important portion, that traversing the

Part I.

In the Calumet Club is preserved the identical hatchet worn by Captain Wells during the last fight, with authenticating documents furnished by James Madison Wolcott, of South Toledo, Ohio, his grandson by his wife Wa-nan-ga-peth (daughter of Me-che-kan-nah-quah or Little Turtle) through his daughter Ah-mah-qua-zah-quah ("A sweet breeze"), who married Judge James Wolcott. It is related that Wa-nan-ga-peth received the news of her husband's death from a stranger Indian who entered, told the message, laid down the hatchet in token of its truth, and departed, unknown as he came.

This narrative of the fight itself, as seen by Mrs. Heald and related to me by her son, is marked by a style of severe simplicity and good faith that seems to command confidence in the mind of the reader. There is no point in the artless story where one is compelled to pause and make a mental allowance for the bias of the narrator, for her excitement and the uncertainty such a state of mind might throw over her accuracy, or even for the errors (save those of omission) which the lapse of years might have caused. All seems natural, unforced and trustworthy. The story goes on:

> In the meantime her horse, which had become excited during the tumult by the smell of blood, commenced prancing around, and an Indian took him by the bit and led him down to the corral, or Indian camp near the fort. [This was on the banks of a slough which entered the river at about where State Street bridge now stands.] Approaching them, an Indian squaw caught sight of the bright-red blanket which was girted on over Mrs. Heald's saddle, for camping purposes, and immediately attempted to take it for her own. Mrs. Heald resisted vigorously, and although one hand was entirely useless and the other badly injured, she took her switch and with it struck the squaw such hard blows that "white welts were raised on her red hide." After this exhibition of spirit, the Indian who had hold of the horse's bit again shouted, "Epeconier! Epeconier!" and it is probably this display of daring which saved Mrs. Heald's life, and perhaps her husband's also.

---

business heart of the city, has been arbitrarily changed to "Fifth Avenue," there being no Fourth or Sixth Avenue adjoining it on either side to excuse the ungrateful, barbarous innovation.

Rebekah Wells Heald was evidently worthy of her name. Daughter of Captain Samuel Wells, niece of Captain William Wells, wife of Captain Nathan Heald, she was a woman whom the sight of blood could not daunt, the smart of wounds weaken, or the fear of bereavement subdue. (For many hours after the battle she supposed herself a widow.) Her son Darius (her mouthpiece in this narrative) was not born until nine years after that dreadful day; and now (1893), in his seventy-third year, he shows the family form and spirit. Tall, stalwart, erect and dignified, he is a typical southern-westerner, a mighty hunter in the past and a tower of patriarchal strength in his old age.

> When she was brought in, after being captured and led down among the Indians, she was stripped of her jewelry—rings, breast-pin, ear-rings and comb. She was badly wounded, and was cared for that night (the fifteenth of August) as tenderly as a sister, by two or three squaws and one French woman, who did everything in their power to relieve her. She saw nothing of her jewelry till the next morning, when a brave made his appearance and pranced around, taking great pains to shew that he was wearing her comb in his scalp-lock—a performance fraught with difficulties, as he had hardly enough hair to keep it in, and found it necessary to push it back from time to time to prevent it from falling to the ground. Poor black Cicely she never saw again.[7] She had perished with the rest. Her horse, too, was gone forever.

This horse was a thoroughbred, the same one that Mrs. Heald, as a bride, had ridden from Kentucky a year before. The Indians had always looked on it with envious eyes, and had employed all means, lawful and otherwise, to get it from the fort. Now it was theirs by conquest, and no later efforts availed to recover it. Doubtless among its new owners its fate was hard and its life short. One winter of starvation, exposure and abuse would "hang its hide on the fence," even while its wretched Indian-pony companions were living on in stubborn endurance.

---

[7] See below.

It turned out afterwards that the Indians took their booty down to Peoria, to sell and "trade" for whisky, and it found its way quickly to St. Louis, where Colonel O'Fallon recognized a great deal as belonging to the Healds, and redeemed it and sent it to Colonel Samuel Wells at the Falls of the Ohio [Louisville] as a memento of his daughter and her husband, both supposed to be dead. It reached there before the Healds did, and the articles are now in possession of the family; most of them were shown by Hon. Darius Heald in Chicago, in 1892, when the before-mentioned short-hand transcript of his mother's story was made, and he and his precious relics were photographed, making a picture hereinafter presented. (See Appendix E.)

The Indian who led Captain Heald down to the camp and claimed him as his prisoner, was a half-breed named Chandonnais. He afterward found that Mrs. Heald was still alive, and, it is supposed, ransomed her from her captor; for, on the morning of the sixteenth, he brought the husband and wife together. He seems to have connived at the escape of both, for they found the matter wonderfully easy—boat and escort at hand and all oversight withdrawn. Years afterward, in 1831, Chandonnais visited the Healds at their home, near O'Fallon, Missouri, and Darius Heald remembers his father's meeting and greeting the brave who had so nobly rescued them. It is thought that the Indians went off down the lake to have "a general frolic"—in other words, torture to death the wounded prisoners.

Here arises before the mind's eye the dim and cloudy vision of horror, the acme of the tragedy, all the more appalling for its shrouding mystery. It makes the flesh creep and the hair stand on end. It sears the heart against the race whereof it was the inborn nature to feel in the eyes a love for the sight of mortal agony, in the ears an eagerness for the shriek of despairing anguish.

The wounded not included! The helpless picked out for torture! The inflamed hurts to be deepened with a pitchfork and perhaps further and mortally inflamed with a burning brand! Kindly Nature's passing lethargy to be quickened into conscious death in frantic anguish!

The twelve militia-men are never again mentioned. They are as if they had never been born, lived and toiled, never volunteered, never served, fought and fell. How is this to be accounted for? Why should their mortality be twice as great as that of the regulars? Darkness hides the answer; but it seems not unlikely that the same hellish ingenuity which held that "the wounded were not included," may also have held that men not wearing the uniform were not protected by the capitulation, and so they perished at the stake, surrounded by the "general frolic" which occupied the savages, good and bad, friendly and inimical, during the flight of the Healds and Kinzies.

There was no place on earth for a race which, through all its history, had found delight in the spectacle of pain, which inflicted torture, not as a means leading to some ulterior object, but as itself a source of joy and gladness. The race is still in existence, but the inhuman part of its characteristics are being refined away, leaving some of its best traits in the more advanced of its present representatives. Later on in this volume mention is made of its standing and its prospects at this time.

Now to take up again the Wau-Bun narrative. The torturing incident, already given, evidently ends the story of Mrs. Helm's personal experiences; all that follows being what others professed to have seen. Yet (possibly by typographical error) the quotation marks, which began with the narration, are continued much further on, including paragraphs wherein she is spoken of in the third person. (See later.) Mrs Helm says:

> The Americans, after the first attack by the Indians, charged upon those who had concealed themselves in a sort of ravine intervening between the sand-banks and the prairie. The latter gathered themselves into a body, and after some hard fighting, in which the number of whites had become reduced to twenty-eight, this little band succeeded in breaking through the enemy and gaining a rising ground not far from the oak woods.
>
> The contest now seemed hopeless, and Lieutenant Helm sent Peresh Leclerc, a half-breed boy in the service of Mr. Kinzie, who had accompanied the detachment and fought manfully on their side, to propose terms of capitulation. It was stipulated that the lives of all the survivors should be spared and a ransom permitted as soon as practicable.

Part I. 21

Lieutenant Helm made the terms of capitulation? How could that be while Captain Heald was present? And what is to be done with Captain Heald's statement of October 7, 1812, less than three months after the event? It reads as follows: "The Indians did not follow me but assembled in a body on the top of the bank, and, after some consultation among themselves, made signs for me to approach them. I advanced toward them alone and was met by one of the Pottowatomie chief called Black Bird, with an interpreter."

The reader will of course choose between the two statements according to his judgement of probabilities and internal evidence of truthfulness. Captain Heald certainly cast no slur on Lieutenant Helm, and appears not even to have entered into the bitterness of feeling against himself and his unhappy surgeon, which seems to have gone on rankling through all the twenty years that elapsed between the direful day and the telling of the story by Mrs. Helm to Mrs. Kinzie.

Mrs. Helm's expression, "Peresh Leclerc, a half-breed boy in the service of Mr. Kinzie who had accompanied the detachment and fought manfully on their side," leaves a possible ambiguity as to whether it is the boy or his master who fought manfully on the side of the whites.

Next follows one of the most noteworthy parts of all Mrs. Helm's narrative, the few words which depict the act of ferocity by which the occasion has been given much of its picturesque and terrible individuality:

> But in the meantime, a horrible scene had been enacted. One young savage, climbing into the baggage-wagon containing the children of the white families, twelve in number, tomahawked the children of the entire group.[8]

This harrowing tale is strongly confirmed by Captain Heald's estimate of losses as given in his letter of Oct. seventh (already quoted), which he states as follows: "Our strength was about fifty-four regulars and twelve militia, out of which twenty-six regulars and twelve militia were killed in action, with two women and twelve children. Ensign George Ronan and

---

[8] See Appendix G for the story of one of the scalped children.

Dr. Isaac V. Van Vorhees, of my company, with Captain Wells of Fort Wayne, to my great sorrow are numbered among the dead. Lieutenant Linai T. Helm, with twenty-five non-commissioned officers and privates, and eleven women and children, were prisoners when we separated."

The next part of Mrs. Helm's narrative is remarkably at variance with the stern, true-seeming and circumstantial account of Captain Wells' death given by Mrs. Heald. Mrs Helm says (following the statement of the slaughter of the innocents):

> This was during the engagement near the sand-hills. When Captain Wells, who was fighting near, beheld it, he exclaimed, "Is that your game, butchering women and children? Then I will kill too!" So saying, he turned his horse's head and started for the Indian camp near the fort, where had been left their squaws and children. Several Indians pursued him as he galloped along. He laid himself flat on the neck of his horse, loading and firing in that position as he would occasionally turn on his pursuers. At length their balls took effect, killing his horse and severely wounding himself. At this moment he was met by Winnemeg and Wauban-see who endeavored to save him from the savages who had now overtaken him. As they supported him along, after having disengaged him from his horse, he received his death blow from another Indian, Pee-so-tum, who stabbed him in the back.

When we observe the incongruities of this tale (not to speak of its contradiction by Mrs. Heald's report) such as the witnessing by Captain Wells of the wagon slaughter (at a time when we know he was far away inland, fighting at the head of the troops); of his alleged dastardly flight from the field toward the Indian camp a mile-and-a-half away, with the avowed intention of killing the squaws and pappooses; his being overtaken on horseback by pursuing enemies on foot; his being held up by two Indians while a third stabbed him in the back, the third being the very one who helped Mrs. Helm to reach the fort; we are only glad to remember that the narrator did not mean to have us understand that she witnessed the occurrences she relates. Internal evidence leads us to suspect that the story came to her from the lips of lying Indians, eager to magnify to Mr. Kinzie their deeds of valor and of kindness, and perhaps justify their treatment of poor Wells, alive and dead. Pee-so-tum may have killed and scalped Wells, but it surely was not under such circumstances as those above set forth. Not even the best friends of the Indian claim for him any appreciation of the virtue of mere veracity. Personal faithfulness of the most touching character he often showed. Even the keeping of promises, often at the cost of great personal sacrifice, has been known as a striking and admirable trait. But "truth for truth's sake" is beyond him—as it is, indeed, beyond the great mass of mankind.

The Wau-Bun story of the experiences of the Kinzie family bears evidences of authenticity and reasonable accuracy, as might be expected from the fact that Mrs. John H. Kinzie probably got it directly from her husband's mother, Mrs. John Kinzie, who was alive at the time when it was first written.

> Those of the family of Mr. Kinzie who had remained in the boat near the mouth of the river were carefully guarded by Kee-po-tah and another Indian. They had seen the smoke, then the blaze, and, immediately after, the report of the tremendous discharge sounded in their ears. Then all was confusion. They realized nothing until they saw an Indian come towards them from the battle-ground leading a horse on which sat a lady, apparently wounded.
>
> "That is Mrs. Heald," cried Mrs. Kinzie. "That Indian will kill her. Run Chandonnais," to one of Mr. Kinzie's clerks, "Take the mule that is tied there and offer it to him to release her."
>
> Her captor by this time was in the act of disengaging her bonnet from her head in order to scalp her. Chandonnais ran up, offered the mule as a ransom, with the promise of two bottles of whisky as soon as they should reach his village. The latter was a strong temptation. "But," said the Indian, "She is badly wounded—she will die—will you give me the whisky at all events?" Chandonnais promised he would, and the bargain was concluded. The savage placed the lady's bonnet on his own head and after an ineffectual effort on the part of some squaws to rob her of her shoes and stockings, she was brought on board the boat, where she lay moaning with pain from the many wounds she had received in both arms.

In this narrative the Indian bargains that he shall have his booty whether the prisoners live or die. This stipulation indicates the savage's view of the value of a prisoner. If likely to live, and therefore exchangeable for ransom, then his life might be spared; if not, then he belonged to his captor and could be used for the keen delight of torture. This is probably the idea which inspired the hellish notion of the exclusion of the wounded from Captain Heald's capitulation. For the unhurt they could get ransom, therefore they would spare their lives. But the wounded! Why spare them? They are not merchantable. Nobody will give anything for a dead man. The dying are available for only one profit—torture.

> When the boat was at length permitted to return to the mansion of Mr. Kinzie, and Mrs. Heald was removed to the house, it became necessary to dress her wounds. Mr. K. applied to an old chief who stood by, and who, like most of his tribe, possessed some skill in surgery, to extract a ball from the arm of the sufferer. "No, father," he replied, "I cannot do it; it makes me sick here," laying his hand on his heart. Mr. Kinzie then performed the operation himself with his penknife.

The discrepancy observable between this account and that of Mrs. Heald herself, which says that on that night she was cared for by squaws in the Indian encampment, may be explained away by supposing that it was on the following day, after the Kinzies had got back to their home on the north bank, that Mrs. Kinzie caught sight of her friend and sent Chandonnais to her rescue in one of the boats they always used for passing and repassing the river, at about where Rush Street bridge now stands. The fact that no mule could well have been tied where the boat lay offshore, near the river's mouth, makes this seem the probable explanation of the incongruity.

At their own mansion the family of Mr. Kinzie were closely guarded by their Indian friends, whose intention it was to carry them to Detroit for security. The rest of the prisoners remained at the wigwams of their captors.

Mrs. Helm, Mr. Kinzie's step-daughter, must have been among those once more housed at the historic building of squared logs built about 1776, by Pointe de Saible. This house was still standing when the village had become, in name at least, a city, which it did in 1837. Mr. Kinzie had planted along its front four poplar trees, and they appear in the early pictures of Chicago. Doubtless, if one were to dig in the open space on the east side of Pine Street, at its junction with Kinzie street, the old roots would be found to this day (1893), and there are probably a hundred living Chicagoans who remember having seen the house itself.

> The following morning, the work of plunder having been completed, the Indians set fire to the fort. A very fair, equitable distribution of the finery appeared to have been made, and shawls, ribbons and feathers fluttered about in all directions. The ludicrous appearance of one young fellow, who had arrayed himself in a muslin gown and the bonnet of one of the ladies, would, under other circumstances, have afforded matter of amusement.
>
> Black Partridge, Wan-ban-see and Kee-po-tah, with two other Indians, having established themselves in the porch of the building as sentinels, to protect the family from any evil the young men might be excited to commit, all remained tranquil for a short space after the conflagration. Very soon, however, a party of Indians from the Wabash made their appearance. These were, decidedly, the most hostile and implacable of all the tribes of the Pottowatomies. Being more remote, they had shared less than some of their brethren in the kindness of Mr. Kinzie and his family, and consequently their sentiments of regard for them were less powerful.

The Wabash Indians must have been smarting with the terrible defeat inflicted on them only about one year before, when General Harrison, whose confidential agent poor Wells had been, fought them at Tippecanoe, on the banks of the Wabash River.

> Runners had been sent to the villages to apprise them of the intended evacuation of the post, as well as of the plans of the Indians assembled to attack the troops. Thirsting to participate in such a scene, they hurried on, and great was their mortification on arriving at the Aux Plaines [Des Plaines River] to meet with a party of their friends bearing with them

Nee-scot-nee-meg badly wounded, and to learn that the battle was over, the spoils divided and the scalps all taken. On arriving at Chicago they blackened their faces and proceeded toward the dwelling of Mr. Kinzie.

From his station on the piazza, Black Partridge had watched their approach, and his fears were particularly awakened for the safety of Mrs. Helm (Mr. Kinzie's step-daughter), who had recently come to the post and was personally unknown to the more remote Indians.[9] By his advice she was made to assume the ordinary dress of a French woman of the country; namely, a short gown and petticoat, with a blue cotton handkerchief wrapped around her head. In this disguise she was conducted by Black Partridge himself to the house of Ouilmette, a Frenchman with a half-breed wife, who formed part of the establishment of Mr. Kinzie, and whose dwelling was close at hand. It so happened that the Indians came first to this house in their search for prisoners. As they approached, the inmates, fearful that the fair complexion and general appearance of Mrs. Helm might betray her for an American, raised a large featherbed and placed her under the edge of it, upon the bedstead, with her face to the wall. Mrs. Bisson, the sister of Ouilmette's wife, then seated herself with her sewing on the edge of the bed. It was a hot day in August, and the feverish excitement of fear and agitation, together with her position, which was nearly suffocating, became so intolerable that at length Mrs. Helm entreated to be released and given up to the Indians.

The words used imply that the step-daughter had not habitually formed part of the family of John Kinzie at Chicago.

"I can but die," said she; "let them put an end to my misery at once."

Mrs. Bisson replied: "Your death would be the destruction of us all, for Black Partridge has resolved that if one drop of the blood of your family is spilled, he will take the lives of all concerned in it, even his nearest friends; and if once the work of murder commences there will be

---

[9] Although this, as well as the earlier part of the account (where Mrs. Helm speaks in the first person) appears in Wau-Bun in continuous quotation marks, it is manifest that the whole later portion is a separate recital. Several interesting anecdotes are given in detail, but for them the reader must look to the delightful original volume which, though not in the market, can be found in the Chicago Historical Society's collection, and also in many private libraries, especially among those Chicagoans who were not burned out in the great fire of 1871. It is to be hoped that some of Mrs. Kinzie's descendants will cause a new edition to be published for the benefit of later comers, who will look to it for amusement (and also instruction) concerning times and scenes so unlike those now around them as to seem to have happened on another planet, instead of on the very soil they tread. (Munsell's Hist. Chic.)

no end of it so long as there remains one white person or half-breed in the country."

This expostulation nerved Mrs. Helm with fresh resolution. The Indians entered, and she could occasionally see them from her hiding-place, gliding about, stealthily inspecting every part of the room, though without making any ostensible search, until, apparently satisfied that there was no one concealed, they left the house.

All this time Mrs. Bisson had kept her seat upon the side of the bed, calmly basting and arranging the patchwork of the quilt on which she was engaged, and preserving the appearance of the utmost tranquility, although she knew not but that the next moment she might receive a tomahawk in her brain. Her self command unquestionably saved the lives of all present.

From Ouilmette's house the party of Indians proceeded to the dwelling of Mr. Kinzie. They entered the parlor, in which the family were assembled with their faithful protectors, and seated themselves upon the floor in silence.

Black Partridge perceived, from their moody and revengeful looks, what was passing in their minds, but he dared not remonstrate with them. He only observed, in a low tone, to Wau-ban-see:

"We have endeavored to save our friends, but it is vain; nothing will save them now."

At this moment a friendly whoop was heard from a party of new-comers on the opposite bank of the river. Black Partridge hastened to meet their leader, as the canoe in which they had hastily embarked touched the bank near the house.

"Who are you?" demanded he.

"A man; who are *you?*"

"A man like yourself; but tell me *who* you are"—meaning, "tell me your disposition, and which side you are for."

"I am the Sau-ga-nash."

"Then make all speed to the house; your friend is in danger and you alone can save him."

Billy Caldwell, the "Sau-ga-nash," or Englishman, was son of Colonel Caldwell, a British officer stationed at Detroit, his mother being a beautiful Pottowatomie girl. He was educated by his father, though serving his mother's race as a chief of the Pottowatomies. (There were always many "chiefs.") He fought under Tecumseh against the whites under Wayne—"Mad Anthony," as he was often called, "Old Tempest," as Caldwell himself calls him[10]—also at the Battle of the Thames, in 1813, when Harrison fought and defeated the combined forces of British and Indians, and the famous chief, Tecumseh, was killed. He took part in the treaty of Greenville, in 1796, and that of Chicago, in 1833; a long space of historic time, covering a racial struggle of many thrilling incidents, not a thousandth part of which can ever see the light. They are buried in blood, smoke, flame and darkness. At this time, it will be observed, Caldwell was an ally of the English.

> Billy Caldwell, for it was he, entered the parlor with a calm step, and without a trace of agitation in his manner. He deliberately took off his accoutrements and planed them, with his rifle, behind the door, and then saluted the hostile savages.
>
> "How now, my friends? A good day to you! I was told there were enemies here, but I am glad to find only friends. Why have you blackened your faces? Is it that you are mourning for those friends you have lost in battle?" (purposely misunderstanding this token of evil designs) "or is it that you are fasting? If so, ask our friend here, and he will give you to eat. He is the Indians' friend, and never yet refused them what they had need of."
>
> Thus taken by surprise, the savages were ashamed to acknowledge their bloody purpose. They therefore said modestly that they came to beg of their friends some white cotton in which to wrap their dead before interring them. This was given to them, with some other presents, and they took their departure peaceably from the premises.

The remainder of both the Wau-Bun and Heald narratives is devoted to the flight from Chicago and the later fate of the fugitives. Before closing this part of my story, I will give the following bit coming from another source.

---

[10] See Appendix H.

Near the (present) north end of State Street bridge stood a log house known to history and tradition as "Cobweb Castle;" a name probably given to it after the rebuilding of the fort in 1816, and after it had become superannuated and superseded. Mrs. Callis, daughter of Mr. Jouett, who came here with him about 1817, says of it: "The house in which my father lived, was built before the massacre of 1812; I know this from the fact that 'White Elk,' an Indian chief, the tallest Indian I ever saw, was frequently pointed out to me as the savage who had dashed out the brains of the children of Sukey Corbin (a camp-follower and washerwoman) against the side of this very house. Mrs. Jouett told her daughter of a frantic mother (perhaps the same Mrs. Corbin), a former acquaintance of hers, who, on that occasion fought the monster all the while the butchery was going on, and who, in her turn, fell a victim herself."

This would indicate that some of the citizens (beside the Kinzies, Healds and Helms) got back to the settlement after the collision at the sand-hills, and that they found at their old homes no sanctuary, no rest, no mercy, no hope.

It is to be observed that, as the Jouetts were not on the spot at the time of the massacre, this part of the story has not the degree of authenticity attaching to the reports of the Healds and Helms. The treaty of 1817 gives, among the Pottowatomie signers, the Indian name of "the White Elk" as "Wa-bin-she-way."

Everything connected with the massacre itself, so far as existing testimony has come to light, has now been told. There is a possibility that one other document may be hidden away; an account written by Lieutenant Helm. But this, if ever found, will necessarily be identical, in all important particulars with the story told by his widow and printed in Wan Bun.[11]

---

[11] Lieutenant (then Captain) Helm is said to have died at or near Bath, Steuben Co., N. Y., about 1817. His widow married, at St. James church, Chicago, in 1836, Dr. Lucius Abbott, of Detroit. Therefore any papers left by the Helms should be sought for in the last named city. Edward G. Mason tells me that there is, or was, among the papers of the Detroit Historical Society, a letter from Lieutenant Helm to Augustus B. Woodward, Esq., at Washington City, in which the writer says that he has nearly completed the history of the Chicago massacre, and that he (Woodward) may expect it in two weeks. The letter was dated Flemington, New Jersey, June 6, 1814. Mr. Mason thinks the letter intimates that the

The day which dawned so bright has dragged through its bloody hours and come to its dark and hideous close. The dead, men, women and children, are at peace. The wounded are suffering the torments of the pit, the rest are shuddering in the uncertainties that lie before them. The Indians are riotously happy; for have they not done harm? Have they not killed, scalped, destroyed, wasted, life and property? Have they not annihilated the source whence they had been getting arms, ammunition and blankets, and driven off the men who tried to keep whisky from them? Have they not made a solitude and called it war? The goods are scattered. The fort is burned. The cattle are dead or dying. The soldiers are defeated, slain or held as prisoners, for ransom if unhurt, for torture if disabled. The babes are brained and their mothers dead or desolate. What more "happy hunting ground" is possible to them this side of hades itself?

In "Wau-Bun," one seems to hear them telling of their individual good deeds and attributing all evil deeds to each other. For the Indian's hand was against every man, even all other Indians. Their bloodiest wars have been between themselves; wars of absolute extermination for the beaten party Every tribe held its lands by conquest and by force. Even if we had taken them by the sword, without compensation (which we never did), they would only have lost their holdings by the selfsame means by which they had gained them.

Well is it for the kindlier folk that the cruel did not stick together. If they had done so, we should be a hundred years in time and a thousand miles in space further back in our territorial progress. But they could not combine. "You might as well try to boil flints into a pudding."

It still remains to me to trace, so far as it is not shrouded in oblivion, the fate of the survivors. But as this leads some distance into the future, I have thought best to treat the matter separately; prefacing the story of what followed the tragedy by a short sketch of what preceded and led up to it. Why did those brave and hapless beings come here? How came they here? What brought their few and scattered footprints to the ground since then trodden by millions?

---

publication of the history may subject the writer to court-martial. Possibly this note may bring to light the lost history in question; a thing much to be desired.

Part I.

The following pages will try to answer these questions, beginning with the very earliest permanent settlement of what is now Chicago.

Part II. Historical and Biographical
How Chicago Began and Who Were Its Beginners

Chapter 1

THE DARK BEFORE THE DAWN

Figure 1. Early Jesuit.

Resolutely, though unwillingly, I pass over the romantic history of the first century of Chicago's annals, the French period beginning about 1678, embracing the thrilling story of La Salle, Marquette and their brave fellow Catholics. Let us take up the tale when, in 1778, during the Revolutionary war; just as the great George Rogers Clark was capturing Indiana, Illinois and in fact the whole Northwest, from the English; one Colonel Arent Schuyler de Peyster (a New York officer of the British army, in command of Fort Mackinac) wrote some doggerel verses which bring Chicago into modern history and literature.[12] In one of his poems he speaks of "Eschikagou" and of Jean Baptiste Pointe de Saible who lived there, and in a footnote he describes the place as "a river and fort at the head of Lake Michigan," and the man as "a handsome negro, well educated, but much in the French interest."

The fort spoken of by Colonel de Peyster, if it had any existence, must have been a mere stockaded trading-post, for neither by English nor by French forces had it been built, and as to American forces, there were none west of the Alleghanies except Clark with his few score of heroic frontiersmen. Fort Dearborn came twenty-six years later, as we shall see.

The word "Chicago" in some of its many forms of spelling[13] had been in recognized existence for a century, being found in the scanty and precious records left by Marquette, La Salle and their contemporaries, though they first call the stream the "Portage River."

Much discussion has arisen about the word and its meaning, but the preponderance of testimony seems to point to the conclusion that the river

---

[12] See appendix A. After the peace. Colonel de Peyster retired to Scotland and lived in or near Dumfries; and it is in his honor that Burns wrote his verses "To Colonel de Peyster," beginning "My honored Colonel, much I feel Thy interest in the poet's weal."

[13] Hurlbut's "Antiquities" discusses the name with great and amusing particularity Here are some of the variations he gives in its spelling and its meaning. Chicagowunzh, the wild onion or leek; (Schoolcraft). Checaqua; a line of chiefs of the Tamaroa Indians, signifying strong. Chigaakwa, "the woods are thin." Checagou, Chicagou, Marquette and La Salle. Shikakok, "at the skunk." Chi-ka-go, wild onion. Chikagou, an Indian chief who went to Paris (before 1752) where the Duchess of Orleans, at Versailles, gave him a splendid snuff box. Chicagou, M. DeLigny in a letter to M. DeSiette. Checaqua, "the Thunder God." Chacaqua, "Divine River." Chicagua or Skunk river (in Iowa). Chicago, skunk, onion or smelling thing; (Gordon S. Hubbard). Chicagoua, equivalent of the Chippewa Jikag; "bête puante." Zhegahg, a skunk. Eschikagou; (Col. De Peyster). Portage de Chegakou. Chikajo. Chi-kaug-ong; (Schoolcraft). Chicazo, corruption of Chickasaw.

took its name from the wild onion, leek or garlick that grew in profusion along its banks in all this region, and is still to be found in many neglected spots of original soil. Bold Tonti, La Salle's faithful lieutenant, speaks of having been nourished during his long tramp from the Illinois River to Green Bay by a weed much like the leek of France, which they dug up with their fingers and ate as they walked—surely the chi-ca-gou.

Figure 2. Little Turtle—Me-Che-Kan-Nah-Quah.

The first official mention of the word "Chicago" was in the "Treaty of Greenville;" a compact made in 1795 between the Indians and "Mad Anthony" Wayne, who had lately whipped them into a treaty-making frame of mind. This treaty placed the boundary line between the whites and the Indians east of the entire state of Indiana, but excepted and retained for trading posts several isolated sections west of the line, among them "one piece of land six miles square at the mouth of Chicago River, emptying into the southwestern end of Lake Michigan, where a fort formerly stood."

"Me-che-kan-nah-quah" or "Little Turtle," who took a prominent part in the making of the treaty, was the father-in-law of William Wells, the hero-martyr of the massacre, as has been set forth in Part I.

Baptiste Pointe de Saible, sometime in the last century, built a log house on the north bank of the Chicago River, near Lake Michigan, just where Pine street now ends. This modest dwelling existed through vicissitudes many and terrible. When built, it stood in a vast solitude. North of it were thick woods which covered the whole of what is now Chicago's proud "North Side." In front of it lay the narrow, deep and sluggish creek which forms the main river; and, with its two long, straggling branches, gives the city its inestimable harbor,[14] with twenty-seven miles of dock frontage. Beyond it, stretching indefinitely southward, lay the grassy flat now the "South Side," the business centre and wealthiest residence portion. Westward, beyond the north and south branches of the river, stretched the illimitable prairie, including what at the present time is the "West Side," the home of manufacturing enterprise and of a population larger than that of the two other portions put together. And to the eastward lay the lake; the only thing in nature which Jean Baptiste could recognize if he should now return to the scene of his long, lonely, half savage, half civilized sojourn.

Suppose him to have built his log dwelling in 1778, the very year when Colonel de Peyster luckily makes a note of his existence; all about him must have been a waste place so far as human occupation is concerned. Bands of roaming Indians from time to time appeared and disappeared. French trappers and voyageurs doubtless made his house their halting-place. Fur-traders' canoes, manned by French "voyageurs," "engages" and "coureurs des bois," paddling the great lakes and unconsciously laying the foundation of the Astor fortunes, called, from time to time, to buy the stores of peltry which he had collected, and leave him the whisky of which he was so fond, but the rest of his time was spent in patriarchal isolation and the society of his Indian wives and their half-breed offspring.

---

[14] The city has, besides, another harbor along the Calumet lake and river, some ten miles to the southward, which, when fully improved, will exceed the first named in extent and value.

The Dark Before the Dawn

Figure 3. General Anthony Wayne. From "Cyclopædia of United States History."—Copyright 1881, by Harper & Brothers.

So far as we know, scarcely a civilized habitation stood nearer than Green Bay on the north, the Vermilion branch of the Wabash on the south and the Mississippi on the west; a tract of nearly fifty thousand square miles.

Pointe de Saible's occupation ended about with the century, when he sold the cabin to one Le Mai. Before this time, however, other settlements had been begun nearer than those above mentioned; and even in the very neighborhood there were a few neighbors. One Guarie had settled on the west side of the North Branch; and Gurdon Hubbard (who came here in 1818) says that that stream was still called "River Guarie" and that he himself saw the remains of corn-hills on what must have been Guarie's farm. (The South Branch was called "Portage River" because it led to the Mud Lake connection with the Des Plaines and so onward to the Mississippi). Pointe de Saible, Le Mai and Guarie have died and left no sign, but there was another pioneer of pioneers in the beginning of the present century who was more lucky. He was Antoine Ouillemette, a Frenchman who took to wife a Pottowatomie squaw and thus obtained a grant of land on part of which the pretty suburb of Wilmette now stands. He did not die till 1829, six years before the final departure of the Pottowatomies for the further West.

Figure 4. William Whistler.

The far-seeing plans which inspired our forefathers in making the treaty of Greenville took shape in 1804, when General Henry Dearborn, Secretary of War under President Jefferson, ordered the building of a fort[15] and a company of soldiers arrived to build it, having marched overland from Detroit under Lieutenant (afterward Colonel) James S. Swearingen. Their Captain, John Whistler, had led an eventful life. Hurlbut in his delightful "Chicago Antiquities" says he was "an officer in the army of the

---

[15] See Appendix B.

Revolution," and adds: "We regret that we have so few facts concerning his history; nor have we a portrait or signature of the patriot." In fact he did serve during the Revolutionary war, but it was on the British side in the army of General Burgoyne, being taken prisoner with the rest, and paroled; joining the American army later in life.[16] With Captain John Whistler came his son, Lieutenant William Whistler, the latter accompanied by his young wife (of her and her daughter we shall hear more hereafter), all of whom came around the lakes on the schooner Tracy. The passengers left the Tracy on arriving at St. Joseph's, Michigan, and came across the lake by a row-boat. When the schooner arrived she anchored outside and her freight was discharged by bateaux, as the river (which made a sharp turn southward just below where Rush Street Bridge now stands and debouched over a shallow bar at about the present foot of Madison Street) was not navigable for lake vessels at that time, or for thirty-one years afterward. Mrs. William Whistler said that some two thousand Indians visited the locality, during the schooner's stay, to see the "big canoe with wings."

We further learn from Mrs. Whistler that there were then in the place but four rude huts or trader's cabins, occupied by white men, Canadian French with Indian wives. She adds:

> "Captain Whistler, upon his arrival, at once set about erecting a stockade and shelter for his protection, followed by getting out the sticks for the heavier work. It is worth mentioning here that there was not at that time, within hundreds of miles, a team of horses or oxen, and as a consequence, the soldiers had to don the harness and, with the aid of ropes, drag home the needed timbers."

This would indicate that the soldiers had made their long march from Detroit (two hundred and eighty miles) without wagons or pack animals to carry tents and rations; or, what is more probable, that the transportation had been hired, and the outfit had returned to Detroit.

---

[16] See Appendix C.

Figure 5. Mrs. William Whistler. From a photograph taken during her visit to Chicago in 1875.

Next steps upon the scene the true pioneer of the Chicago of to-day; John Kinzie.[17] This first of citizens had learned of the proposed establishment of the military post, Fort Dearborn, and, foreseeing with his usual boldness and sagacity the advantages to spring from it, had come over from his residence on the St. Joseph's river, and bought from Le Mai the old Pointe de Saible log-cabin. Shortly after the establishment of the fort he brought his family to the place wherein the name of Kinzie has been always most distinguished. The family consisted of his wife, Eleanor (Lytle), widow of a British officer named McKillip, her young daughter

---

[17] See Appendix D.

Margaret, who afterward became Mrs. Lieutenant Helm, and an infant son, John Harris Kinzie. They occupied the old North Side log-house up to 1827—about twenty-five years—(except from 1812 to 1816, the years of desolation) and it stood for more than ten years longer; a landmark remembered by scores if not hundreds of the Chicagoans of this time (1893).

For much of our scanty knowledge concerning the years following the building of the fort we are indebted to Mrs. Julia (Ferson) Whistler, wife of William and therefore daughter-in-law of John, the old Burgoyne British regular.[18]

From 1804 to 1811, the characteristic traits of this far away corner of the earth were its isolation; the garrison within the stockade and the ever present hovering clouds of savages outside, half seen, half trusted, half feared; its long summers, (sometimes hot and sometimes hotter); and its long winters, (sometimes cold and sometimes colder); its plenitude of the mere necessaries of life, meat and drink, shelter and fuel, with utter destitution of all luxuries; its leisurely industry and humble prosperity; Kinzie, the kindly link between the red man and the white, vying with the regular government agent in the purchase of pelts and the sale of rude Indian goods. In 1805 Charles Jouett was the United States Indian Agent here. He was a Virginian, son of one of the survivors of Braddock's defeat. How much of his time was spent here and how much elsewhere we do not know. In Mrs. John H. Kinzie's charming book "Wau-Bun" he is not even mentioned, which circumstance suggests that his relations with old John Kinzie were not cordial; a state of things to be expected, considering their relative positions. He was an educated man and must have enjoyed the friendship of Jefferson, Madison and Monroe, judging by his appointment as Government Agent, first at Detroit, later at Chicago (1804), which latter post he resigned in 1811, only to be reappointed in 1817.

It is probable that the United States agent was at a disadvantage in dealing with the Indians, as he would have to obey the law forbidding the supplying them with spirits; which law the other traders ignored. In

---

[18] See Appendix C.

Hurlbut's "Antiquities" a bit of "local color" gives with much vividness the condition of the prairie in those days.

Figure 6. Charles Jouett.

"In the holidays of 1808-9 Mr. Jouett (then a widower) married Susan Randolph Allen of Kentucky, and they made their wedding journey on horseback in January, through the jungles, over the snow drifts, on the ice and across the prairies, in the face of driving storms and the frozen breath of the winds of the north. They had, on their journey, a negro servant named Joe Battles and an Indian guide whose name was Robinson; possibly the late chief Alexander Robinson. A team and wagon followed, conveying their baggage, and they marked their route for the benefit of any future travelers."

The government had tried to befriend the Indian in every way. It did not forbid private traders from dealing with him; but it appointed agents whose duty it was to sell him goods at prices barely sufficient to cover cost and expenses. At the same time it forbade, under penalty, the supplying him with liquor in any quantity, upon any pretext. Unhappily the last-named kindly effort thwarted the first. The miserable savage loved the venal white who would furnish him with the poison. For it he would give not only his furs, but his food and shelter, his wives and children, his body and his everlasting soul. As the grand old Baptist missionary Isaac McCoy says, regarding the treaty of 1821, at which he was present:

"At the treaty Topenebe, the principal chief of the Pottowatomies, a man nearly eighty years of age [a long and constant friend of the Kinzies], irritated by the continued refusal on the part of the commissioners to gratify his importunities for whisky, exclaimed in the presence of his tribe: 'We care not for the land, the money or the goods. It is whisky we want. Give us the whisky.' After the business of the treaty was concluded and before the Indians left the treaty grounds, seven barrels of whisky were given them, and within twenty-four hours afterward ten shocking murders were committed amongst them."

To quote from Munsell's *History of Chicago*:

> Few and meagre are the records of occurrences on the banks of the Chicago during these quiet years. The stagnation in this remote corner of creation was in sharp contrast with the doings in the great world, for these were the momentous Napoleonic years. Austerlitz, Jena, Eylau, Friedland, Wagram, were fought between 1805 and 1809, and one wonders whether even the echoes of the sound of those fights reached little Fort Dearborn. Yet the tremendous doings were not without their influence; for it was Napoleon's "European System" and England's struggle against it that precipitated our war of 1812; and one trivial incident in that war was the ruin of our little outpost.

The incidents of daily life went on in the lonely settlement, as elsewhere.

There was the occasional birth of a baby in the Kinzie house, the fort or somewhere about, as there were several women here, soldiers' wives, etc. Those born in the Kinzie mansion and the officers' families we know about. But these were not all. There were at least a dozen little ones who first saw the light in this locality, whose play-ground was the parade and the river bank, whose merry voices must have added a human sweetness to this savage place; whose entire identity, even to their names, is lost. The one thing we know about them is how they died, and that has been told in Part I.

Chapter 2

BUILDING OF THE FIRST FORT DEARBORN

Figure 7. A "red-coat" of 1812.

Delaying our narrative for a moment, we here bring upon the scene another figure—the most distinguished and heroic of all who were to play a part in the terrific tragedy which formed its climax—William Wells.[19] This brave fellow, born of white parents, but early stolen by Indians, and only restored after arriving at manhood, was a friend and agent of General Harrison, who was at that time Governor of the Indian Territory. Captain Wells had come to Chicago in 1803 on official duty, as appears by a license (which the writer has had the privilege of inspecting) issued to Jean B. La Geuness, to trade with the Indians. This paper is still in existence, in the possession of Dr. H. B. Tanner of Kaukaunee, Wis., having come to him from among the papers of Judge John Lawe of Green Bay, who was for many years agent of the American (John Jacob Astor's) Fur Company. The license bears the name of "William Henry Harrison, Governor of the Indian Territory and Superintendent of Indian Affairs," and is signed "by order of the Governor. William Wells, Agent at Indian Affairs, Chicago, August the 30th, 1803."

This license must have been signed in the old De Saible house. No fort was here yet, nor any government office or officer, so far as we know. Indeed, this page records, for the first time in history, the fact that William Wells was in Chicago before 1812. Eight years later his niece was to appear on the scene, arriving as the bride of Captain Heald, then commanding Fort Dearborn.

But to return to Captain Whistler and the embryo fort.

A glimpse of early garrison-life appears in the personal narrative of Captain Thomas C. Anderson, published in Volume IX of the Wisconsin Historical Collection:

> During my second year [1804-5] at Min-na-wack, or Mill-wack-ie [Milwaukee] Captain Whistler, with his company of American soldiers, came to take possession of Chicago. At this time there were no buildings here except a few dilapidated log huts covered with bark. Captain Whistler had selected one of these as a temporary, though miserable, residence for his family, his officers and men being under canvas. On

---

[19] See Appendix E.

Building of the First Fort Dearborn 49

being informed of his arrival I felt it my duty to pay my respects to the authority so much required by the country. On the morrow I mounted Kee-ge-kaw, or Swift-goer, and the next day I was invited to dine with the Captain. On going to the house, the outer door opening into the dining-room, I found the table spread, the family and guests seated, consisting of several ladies, all as jolly as kittens.

The fort consisted of a stockade large enough to contain a parade-ground and all the fort buildings, officers' quarters, barracks, offices, guard-house, magazine, etc., and also two block-houses, each built so that the second story overhung the lower, thus giving a vertical fire for musketry to guard against an enemy's setting fire to the house. One of these was at the southeast corner and the other at the northwest. There were entrances on the south side (Michigan Avenue), and on the north or water side, where a sunken road led down to the river. Mr. Blanchard, in his "Chicago and the Northwest," says that the armament consisted of the musket and bayonet, and three pieces of light artillery—probably the old six-pounder, which threw a round ball about double the size of a child's fist.

Figure 8. Fort Dearborn, 1803-4. (Fergus' Series, No. 16)

Beside the fort, the government put up an "Agency House," which stood on the river bank just west of the sunken road that led from the fort to the water. Mrs. Kinzie describes this building as an old-fashioned log-house with a hall running through the middle, and one large room on each side. Piazzas extended the whole length of the building, in front and rear. It played a part in the final tragedy, and was destroyed with the fort on August 15, 1812.

Munsell's "History of Chicago" gives the following picture at and after the building of the first fort:

> When the schooner Tracy set sail and slowly vanished in the northwestern horizon, we may fancy that some wistful glances followed her. For those left behind it was the severing of all regular ties with "home," for years or forever. An occasional courier from Detroit or Fort Wayne brought news from the outside world; a rare canoe or bateau carried furs to Mackinaw and brought back tea, flour, sugar, salt, tobacco, hardware, powder and lead, dry goods, shoes, etc., perhaps a few books[20] and, best of all, letters! But between-times, what had they to make life worth living? Which of the compensations kind Nature always keeps in store, for even the most desolate of her children, were allotted to them?
>
> They had the lake for coolness and beauty in summer; the forest for shelter, warmth and cheer in winter; masses of flowers in spring, and a few—very few—fruits and nuts in autumn, such as wild grapes and strawberries, wintergreen-berries, cranberries, whortleberries, hazel-nuts, walnuts, hickory-nuts, beech-nuts, etc. There was no lack of game to be had for the hunting, or fish for the catching. The garrison had cattle, therefore there was doubtless fresh beef, milk and butter. So a "good provider," as John Kinzie doubtless was (we know that he was the soul of hospitality) would be certain to keep his wife's larder always full to overflowing.
>
> The garrison officers' families made company for each other and the Kinzies and Jouetts; the soldiers gave protection and a thousand other services to all, and the two fifers and two drummers made music—such

---

[20] John H. Kinzie used to tell how, as a boy, he learned to read from a spelling-book which was unexpectedly found in a chest of tea, and that books were associated with the smell of tea in his mind forever after.

as it was. This rude melody was not all they had, however, for John Kinzie was a fiddler as well as a trader and a silver-smith ("Shaw-nee-aw-kee," or the "silver-smith," was his Indian name), and in the cool summer evenings, sitting on his porch, would send the sound of his instrument far and wide, over river and plain, through the dewy silence of the peaceful landscape.

They had love and marriage, birth and death, buying and selling and getting gain; and, happily, had not the gift of "second sight," to divine what lay before them; what kind of end was to come to their exile.

Mr. Wentworth's Fort Dearborn speech (Fergus' Historical Series No. 16, page 87) quotes a letter he had received from Hon. Robert Lincoln, Secretary of War under President Garfield. From it we learn that no muster-roll of the garrison at Fort Dearborn in 1811 or 1812 is on file at the War Department, but that the general returns of the army show that the fort was garrisoned from June 4, 1804, to June, 1812, by a company of the First Regiment of Infantry. In these returns the strength of the garrison, officers, musicians and privates, is given as follows: Under Captain John Whistler, June 4, 1804, 69; Dec. 31, 1806, 66; Sept. 30, 1809, 77. Under Captain Nathan Heald, Sept. 30, 1810, 67; Sept. 30, 1811, 51, and June —, 1812, 53.[21]

The deficiency of records in the archives of the War Department may perhaps be accounted for by the fact that the British, after the so-called "battle" of Bladensburgh, took Washington and burned all the government buildings.

In 1811 Captain Nathan Heald, then in command of Fort Dearborn, went down to Kentucky, where he married Rebekah Wells daughter of Captain Samuel Wells and niece of William.[22] The newly married pair came up overland (probably following the trail marked by Mr. Jouett), bringing the wedding treasures of the bride—silver, etc., and her own personal adornments, which interesting relics, after vicissitudes strange and

---

[21] See Appendix B for a muster-roll dated Dec 31, 1810 (the latest entry which gives names), wherein are shown several who appear later as victims of the massacre.
[22] See Appendix E for additional details regarding the romantic history of the Wells and Heald families.

terrible, are now in possession of her son, Darius Heald, and, with him, are depicted elsewhere in these pages.

Mrs. Heald's narrative of these events, as reported to me by her son, is as follows:

> In the summer of 1811, Captain Heald, then in command of Fort Dearborn, at Chicago, got leave of absence to go down to Louisville, to get married. He went on horseback, alone, traveling by compass.
>
> They were married, and after the wedding started north on horseback for Fort Dearborn. There were four horses—two for the bride and groom, one for the packs and blankets, and one for a little negro slave-girl named Cicely. This girl had begged so hard to be brought along that they could not refuse her request, although it was, as the Captain said, adding one more to the difficulties of making the long, lonesome, toilsome trip on horseback. They traveled by compass, as before. The horses were good ones, and not Indian ponies. Those that the Captain and his bride rode were thoroughbreds, as was the one ridden by the slave-girl, and they had also a good one to carry the pack, so that they made the trip in about a week's time; starting Thursday, and reaching Fort Dearborn on the following Wednesday night, making about fifty miles a day. Nothing of importance occurred on the bridal trip; they arrived safely, and the garrison turned out to receive them with all the honors of war, the bride being quite an addition to the little company.
>
> Rebekah was much pleased with her reception, and found everything bright and cheerful. She liked the wild place, the wild lake and the wild Indians; everything suited her ways and disposition, "being on the wild order herself," she said; and all went on very pleasantly. Among other gayeties there was skating in winter up and down the frozen river, and Ensign Ronan was a famous skater. Sometimes he would take an Indian squaw by the hands, she holding her feet still, and swing her back and forth from side to side of the little stream, until he came to a place where there was a deep snowdrift on the bank, when he would (accidentally, of course) loose his grip on her hands, and she would fly off into the snowdrift and be buried clear out of sight.

In 1812 the peaceful quiet was rudely startled, then assaulted, then destroyed. The first breach of the peace was the killing by Mr. Kinzie (in self-defense) of one John Lalime, Indian interpreter at Fort Dearborn.[23] This was early in 1812. It had, however, nothing to do with the friendliness or enmity of the red-men.

The second event was of a different kind. A man named Lee,[24] who lived on the lake-shore, near the fort, had enclosed and was farming a piece of land on the northwest side of the South Branch, within the present "Lumber District," about half way between Halsted Street and Ashland avenue. It was first known as "Lee's Place," afterwards as "Hardscrabble." It was occupied by one Liberty White, with two other men and a boy, the son of Mr. Lee.

Figure 9. Cabin in the Woods.

---

[23] See Appendix F.
[24] This name I find sometimes spelled "Lee," and sometimes "See."

This spot was not far from the place where Père Marquette passed the winter of 1674-75; perhaps the very same ground. (See Munsell's History of Chicago for a copy of the good Father's journal, with parallel translation.) Mrs. John Kinzie, first in a pamphlet dated in 1836, and published in 1844, and later in Wau-Bun, gives an extremely picturesque account of the alarm, evidently taken down from the lips of those who had been present; namely her husband (then a boy), his mother, Mrs. John Kinzie, and his half-sister, Mrs. Helm.

It was the evening of the 7th of April, 1812. The children of Mrs. Kinzie were dancing before the fire to the music or their father's violin. The tea-table was spread, and they were awaiting the return of their mother, who was gone to visit a sick neighbor. [Mrs. John Burns, living at about where is now the crossing of Kinzie and State Streets, had just been delivered of a child.] Suddenly their sports were interrupted; the door was thrown open and Mrs. Kinzie rushed in pale with terror, and scarcely able to articulate.

"The Indians! The Indians!"

"The Indians! What? Where?"

"Up at Lee's place, killing and scalping!"

With difficulty Mrs. Kinzie composed herself sufficiently to give the information that while she was up at Burns's a man and a boy were seen running down with all speed to the opposite side of the river; that they called across to give notice to Burns's family to save themselves, for the Indians were at Lee's place, from which they had just made their escape. Having given this terrifying news they made all speed for the fort, which was on the same side of the river that they were. All was now consternation and dismay. The family were hurried into two old pirogues [dug-out tree-trunks] that were moored near the house, and paddled with all possible haste across the river to take refuge in the fort.

Mrs. Kinzie goes on to give the fullest account we have of this initial murder, fitting prelude to the bloody drama to follow a few months later. Here is a condensation of her narrative:

In the afternoon a party of ten or twelve Indians, dressed and painted, arrived at the Lee house, and according to their custom, entered and seated themselves without ceremony. Something in their appearance and manner excited the suspicions of one of the family, a Frenchman [Debou], who remarked: "I don't like the looks of those Indians; they are not Pottowatomies." Another of the family, a discharged soldier, said to a boy (a son of Lee): "If that is the case, we had better get away if we can. Say nothing, but do as you see me do." As the afternoon was far advanced, the soldier walked leisurely toward the two canoes tied near the bank. They asked where he was going. He pointed to the cattle which were standing among the hay-stacks on the opposite bank, and made signs that they must go and fodder them and then return and get their supper.

Figure 10. Kinzie Mansion—1812.

He got into one canoe and the boy into the other. When they gained the opposite side they pulled some hay for the cattle, and when they had gradually made a circuit so that their movements were concealed by the hay-stacks, they took to the woods and made for the fort. They had run a quarter of a mile when they heard the discharge of two guns successively. They stopped not nor stayed until they arrived opposite Burns's place (North State and Kinzie streets), where they called across to warn the Burns family of their danger, and then hastened to the fort.

A party of soldiers had that afternoon obtained leave to go up the river to fish. The commanding officer ordered a cannon to be fired to warn them of their danger. Hearing the signal they took the hint, put out their torches and dropped down the river as silently as possible. It will be remembered that the battle of Tippecanoe, the preceding November, had rendered every man vigilant, and the slightest alarm was an admonition to "beware of Indians."

When the fishing-party reached Lee's place, it was proposed to stop and warn the inmates. All was still as death around the house. They groped their way along, and as the corporal jumped over the small enclosure he placed his hand on the dead body of a man. By the sense of touch he soon ascertained that the head was without a scalp and was otherwise mutilated. The faithful dog of the murdered man stood guarding the remains of his master.

Captain Heald, writing from the fort, gives a shorter statement, adding some further particulars:

> Chicago, April 15, 1812.—The Indians have commenced hostilities in this quarter. On the sixth instant, a little before sunset, a party of eleven Indians, supposed to be Winnebagoes, came to Messrs. Russell and See's cabin, in a field on the Portage branch of the Chicago River, about three miles from the garrison, where they murdered two men; one by the name of Liberty White, an American, and the other a Canadian Frenchman whose name I do not know. [Debou.] White received two balls through his body, nine stabs with a knife in his breast, and one in his hip, his throat was cut from ear to ear, his nose and lips were taken off in one piece, and his head was skinned almost as far round as they could find any hair. The Frenchman was only shot through the neck and scalped. Since the murder of these two men, one or two other parties of Indians have been lurking about us, but we have been so much on our guard they have not been able to get any scalps.

Among all the tribes of savages met by various immigrations of Europeans, a thousand differences of arms, implements, manners, habits and customs were observed. Some were more barbarous, others less; but there was one trophy one weapon, one trait, invariable and universal—the bleeding scalp, the sharp scalping-knife, the rage for scalping.

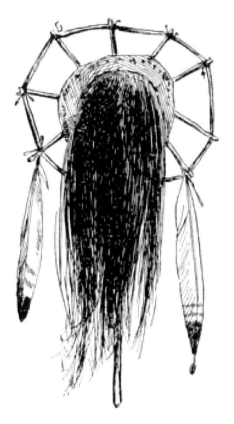

Figure 11. Human Scalp.

This proves much. It shows that killing was not a mere means to an end, but the end aimed at. It shows that sheer, unadulterated, unmitigated murder was the ideal grace of manhood. The brain-pan of man, woman or child yielded its covering, torn away warm and quivering, and the possessor was sure of the honor and favor of his fellows, men, women and children. No woman shed a tear over the locks of a sister woman; no child over the curls of a baby.

Savagery the world has ever known, and isolated instances of wholesale destruction of non-combatants in the drunkenness of victory; but there is no record of a whole race, consisting of many tribes, spread over many lands, enduring for many generations, where such diabolism was the general ethnic trait.

Chapter 3

ENGLISH AND INDIAN SAVAGES

Figure 12. Indian Warrior.

The Winnebagoes, we observe, are charged by Captain Heald with this outbreak of lawlessness.

The Pottowatomies always averred that they had nothing to do with the great massacre, and this may be true of the tribe as a whole, but it is well known that many of its members, as well as the Winnebagoes, had been engaged with the Ottawas and Shawnees at the battle of Tippecanoe, less than a year before. The English, ever since the Revolution, had been seeking their friendship—and our injury—by giving them yearly presents at Maiden (in Canada, near Detroit), and they placed much foolish reliance on the red-men's help in prosecuting the war of 1812. Foolish, because the unspeakable savage was only formidable in sneaking hostilities against women and children, and against men unwarned and overmatched; not in a fair fight on equal terms. In all that contest they were simply murderously hostile. Wau-Bun gives an incident which displays their animus. In the spring of 1812 two Indians of the Calamic (Calumet) band came to the fort to visit Captain Heald. One of them, Nau-non-gee, seeing Mrs. Heald and Mrs. Helm playing battle-door on the parade-ground, said to the interpreter (probably John Kinzie): "The white chief's wives are amusing themselves very much; it will not be long before they will be hoeing in our cornfields."

The service they rendered England is such as England should blush to receive. It was the service of inspiring terror in the hearts of the helpless. Two days after the massacre at Chicago, the unfortunate and execrated General Hull surrendered Detroit to the British and Indians. Why did he do so? He had suffered no defeat. He could have crossed the river and fought them with every prospect of victory. But could he leave that town at the mercy of fiends who knew no mercy? He could have given battle at Detroit itself, but the British General (Proctor) kindly told him that if he should be compelled to assault he would not be able to control his Indian allies. Now, in case of defeat, Hull's army could take care of themselves, either as prisoners or fugitives; but what might become of a thousand helpless, hapless women and children, and the wounded men he would have on his hands? What would have become of them? Read further on in this narrative and see!

So, in an evil hour for himself. General Hull took the merciful course, and innocent blood was spared. The fall of Detroit was directly due to non-military caution, a mercifulness that had nothing to do with the hazard of civilized war and the fate of the army. The unfortunate commander, a man of undoubted courage, a man who had served his country through the Revolution, was tried by court-martial and condemned to death. The sentence was not carried out in form, but in substance it was, for he lived in obscurity, if not obloquy, and died with a stained name which is slowly recovering its proper place.

Vain is it for apologists to try to shift on to local subordinates the blame for the shameful course of Lord Liverpool's government. The same king was (nominally) reigning who had employed these same allies only thirty years before, George Third was on the throne through both wars; that of the Revolution and that of 1812. English ears—such as were sensitive to just and bitter denunciation—must still, in 1812, have been ringing with the public outcry against the infamy of 1775-82. Even England's own servants protested against it. Doubtless they felt, as any gentleman must feel, that he who stays at home in personal safety and employs base minions to do his murdering, is more contemptible than are the minions themselves, for they at least take their lives in their hands when they set out.

Where stand the guilty in this business? Lower than where we should stand if we had, during our Civil War, incited the negroes to the destruction of their masters' families, for the negro cannot be as cruel as the Indian could not helping being. Lower than Russia would stand if, in a war along the Afghan frontier, she should scheme for a new Sepoy rebellion, with its ravishing and maiming of well born English women. Such women were treated worse than even Dante's fancy could portray, and yet not worse than were the survivors of the Chicago Massacre.

In the little settlement a wild season of alarm followed the double murder at Hardscrabble. The surviving civilians, consisting of a few discharged soldiers and some families of half-breeds, organized themselves for defense. They took for their stronghold the Agency House already-mentioned as standing on the river-bank just west of the fort. The house (as has been said) was built of logs and had porches on both its long sides. They planked up the porches, leaving loopholes for firing through, and set guards in proper military fashion. To quote once more from Munsell.

>As this was outside of garrison duty, it must have required a volunteer force, organized and armed; and this seems to furnish a clue hitherto unmarked by any historian, to explain the presence of "twelve militia" who were mentioned by Captain Heald in his report as having taken part in the fight of August 15th, and as having been every one killed. No other mention of these devoted twelve exists in any form except the grim memorandum of death at the post of duty.[25] Evidently they must have been organized and armed under the auspices of the government force at this time, from the discharged soldiers and half-breeds, and perhaps included Lee, Pettell, Burns, Russell, etc., all of whom were probably enrolled and expected pay from the government, albeit their claim necessarily lapsed with their own death on that bloody day. In confirmation of this suggestion we have Mrs. Kinzie's remark (Wau-Bun, p. 244) that Lee, his son, and all his household, except his wife and daughter, had perished in the affray. Also her mention of Mrs. Burns and her infant among the survivors; no word being uttered about the husband and father.
>
>The Kinzies did not return to their North Side house. Mr. Kinzie had succeeded Lalime as government interpreter, and doubtless the garrison needed his services almost continually. There were several slight alarms and disturbances. A night patrol fired at a prowling red-man, and a hatchet hurled in return missed its mark and struck a wagon-wheel. A horse-stealing raid upon the garrison stables, failing to find the horses, was turned into an attack on the sheep, which were all stabbed and set loose. These alarms and other things combined to show that the quiet of the preceding days had come to an end. The unspeakable Indian had been bribed, tempted and misled by the miserable Englishman to take up again his cruelties; his burning, scalping, tomahawking, knifing and mutilation of combatants and non-combatants alike, men, women and children.

---

[25] See Mrs. Kinzie's narrative and Captain Heald's letter, hereinafter quoted.

War was declared by the United States against England on June 12, 1812. Mackinaw was taken by the British on July 16. Having Detroit to protect and a force of British and Indians to oppose, General Hull naturally aimed to mass his forces and abandon all indefensible outlying posts, such as Fort Dearborn evidently was. Therefore, about August 1st, he sent by Winnemeg, a friendly Indian, a dispatch to Captain Heald, ordering him to evacuate the fort and to proceed to Detroit by land with his command, leaving it to his discretion to dispose of the public property as he might think proper.[26] Mrs. Kinzie, in Wau-Bun, says that the messenger arrived on August 7th, instead of the 9th which Captain Heald names as the date of his receipt of the order, and adds that the same letter brought news of the declaration of war (which had taken place about two months earlier) and of the loss of the post at Mackinaw. She also gives us a new reading of the dispatch, quite different from that given by Captain Heald. She says the orders to Captain Heald were "to vacate the fort if practicable, and in that event to distribute all the United States property contained in the fort and in the United States factory, or agency, among the Indians in the neighborhood." This discrepancy between our two sources of information becomes important in judging of the blame, if any, attributable to Captain Heald for the disaster toward which all were hastening. Guided by the ordinary rules of evidence, we must take Captain Heald's version as the true one, and believe that the order was peremptory, only to be disobeyed if the subordinate officer felt sure that it would not have been given if his superior had been on the spot; and also that the distribution of goods was, on Captain Heald's part, a voluntary concession intended to win the favor of the Indian—the incurable savage.

It should here be stated that there is a broad divergence—one might say a contradiction—between the Kinzie account and the Heald account of the occurrences of that troubled, appalling, disastrous time. Mrs. Kinzie says that Winnemeg privately told Mr. Kinzie that the fort ought not to be evacuated, seeing that it was well supplied with provisions and ammunition, and advised waiting for reinforcements. Also that if Captain

---

[26] See Appendix E.

Heald was to go at all, he should start at once, to get out of the way of the hostiles by a forced march while the Indians were dividing the spoil. (How many "forced marches" would it have taken to make that lumbering caravan safe from pursuit by the red runners of the wilds?) She says:

> The order for evacuating the post was read next morning upon parade. It is difficult to understand why Captain Heald, in such an emergency, omitted the usual form of calling a council of war with his officers. It can only be accounted for by the fact of a want of harmonious feeling between himself and one of his junior officers—Ensign Ronan, a high-spirited and somewhat overbearing, but brave and generous young man.

A "council of war" between the captain and his two lieutenants and (perhaps) the surgeon, to debate an unconditional order received from the general commanding the division, does not strike the average reader as an "usual form," nor does any disaffection on the part of the junior among the officers seem likely to enter into the question, one way or the other. But the suggestion throws a side-light on the unhappy state of things at Fort Dearborn. It seems unquestionable that this young ensign was not in accord with his captain, and that the Kinzies, especially the young story-teller, Mrs. Helm (who was Mrs. Kinzie's authority), sided with the junior—as was perhaps natural. To quote from Munsell:

> It becomes necessary here to call to mind the possible bias which may have existed in the hearts of the narrators in handing down the story to Mrs. Kinzie, the writer of Wau-Bun, who probably never saw the principal actor in it, John Kinzie, behaving died two years before her marriage with his son, John H. Kinzie. The latter was only nine years old at the time of the massacre. His mother, however, Mrs. Kinzie, she did know well, also his aunt, Mrs. Helm [John's step-daughter], from whose lips the Wau-Bun account of the massacre was taken down by her. It is quite certain that departure meant ruin to John Kinzie; for of all the property he had accumulated in his long, able, arduous and profitable business life, not a handful could be carried away by land. And the event showed that he, personally, had nothing to fear from the Indians.

Here is what Mrs. Heald says about these matters:

It is all false about any quarrel between Ronan and Captain Heald. The ensign thought the world of the captain, and gave him a big book with their two names written it. Among the property recovered after the massacre was this book, which the Indians thought was the Bible. They would pass their hands across the pages and point significantly heavenward; but in fact the book was a dictionary and is still in possession of the family, having been bound in buckskin to preserve such part as has not already succumbed to the many vicissitudes. Occasionally Indians would come and steal horses when the men were some distance away cutting hay for the winter's supplies, and they were apt to try to get the scalp of any white person against whom they had any hard feeling.

Mrs. Heald recalls a particular case where a soldier, a great stammerer, was out on picket, and from the block-house window she saw an Indian try to get between him and the fort. To attract the soldier's attention Captain Heald had a gun fired, and the man, when he saw his peril, started homeward, the Indian at the same time starting to cut him off. The soldier was the best runner, and when the Indian called out to him some taunting expression, he looked over his shoulder and tried to shout a retort, but his stuttering tongue made this take so long that he came near losing his life, though at last he got in safely.

In writing the story of the events of that eventful time, there being but two sources of information—to some extent divergent, even contradictory—one is tempted to print them in parallel columns and let the reader take his choice. Each has the same degree of authenticity, seeing that Mrs. Helm, an actor in the tragedy, told Mrs. Kinzie the story, who gives it to us; while Mrs. Heald, also an actor (and besides, a badly wounded sufferer), told it often to her son, the Hon. Darius Heald, who gives it to us. But as the parallel columns might prove more controversial than interesting, the plan I have pursued is the presenting of undisputed facts, and, in case of controversy, the account which seems most probable, with the adverse side when necessary.

66 *Joseph Kirkland*

NOTE

The Heald story is now for the first time made a part of permanent history. In 1891, while writing the "Story of Chicago," I learned that Darius Heald, son of Nathan and Rebekah [Wells] Heald, was still living; whereupon I got him to come to Chicago from his home in Missouri, bringing all the relics and mementoes of his parents which he could find. He came, and sat for a portrait with the relics by his side, and his entire story was taken down in short-hand from his own lips. The little which was available is included in my "Story of Chicago," and the remainder I caused to be published in the Magazine of American History. (See Appendix E.)

Figure 13. George Third.

Chapter 4

A LONG FAREWELL

The departure was not approved by all, if any, of the subordinate officers. It was urged on Capt. Heald that the command would be attacked; that the attack would have been made long before if it had not been for the Indians' regard for the Kinzies; that the helplessness of the women and children and the invalided and superannuated soldiers was sure to make the march slow and perilous, and that the place could well be defended. Captain Heald pleaded his orders, and alleged that the place was not provisioned to stand a siege.

Upon one occasion, as Captain Heald was conversing with Mr. Kinzie on the parade, he remarked: "I could not remain, even if I thought best, for I have but a small store of provisions." "Why, captain," said a soldier who stood nearby, forgetting all etiquette, "you have cattle enough to last the troops six months." "But I have no salt to preserve it with." "Then jerk it," said the man, "as the Indians do their venison."[27] (Wau-Bun.)

Captain Heald, in his letter of November 7th, 1812 (less than three months after the massacre), says of the Indians: "The neighboring Indians got the information as early as I did, and came in from all quarters in order to receive the goods in the factory store, which they understood were to be given them. The collection was unusually large for that place, but they conducted with the strictest propriety until after I left the fort." But Wau-Bun gives a different coloring to the matter, and with such circumstantiality that there seems necessarily to be some truth on the other side. Mrs. Kinzie says that there was dissatisfaction in the garrison amounting to insubordination (as instanced by the soldier's interference in the captain's talk with Mr. Kinzie) and increasing insolence on the part of the Indians. The story runs:

> Entering the fort in defiance of the sentinels, they made their way without ceremony to the officers' quarters. On one occasion an Indian took up a rifle and fired it in the parlor of the commanding officer, as an expression of defiance. Some were of the opinion that this was intended among the young men as a signal for an attack. The old chiefs passed backwards and forwards among the assembled groups with the appearance of the most lively agitation, while the squaws rushed to and fro in great excitement and evidently prepared for some fearful scene. (Wau-Bun.)

---

[27] This is done by cutting the meat in thin slices and placing it on a scaffold over a fire, which dries the meat and smokes it at the same time.

Figure 14. Squaw.

(As might be expected, the squaws often showed themselves the most bitter, cruel and relentless partisans.)

The feeling will intrude itself that Captain Heald was too truthful, trustful, brave and good a man to be a perfect Indian-fighter. He had none of the savage's traits except his courage. He was without guile, or craft, or duplicity or cruelty. The soul of honor, he attributed good faith to his foe. A temperate man, he could not conceive of the insanity of maniacs to whom the transient delirium of drunkenness is heaven on earth.

We must remember that there is always a hard feeling between the military and the civil authority in every Indian post—East Indian or American Indian—the soldier holding the sword and the civilian the purse, each slightly envying the other what he possesses, and slightly despising him for the lack of what he is deprived of.

At any rate. Captain Heald (by and with the advice of Mr. Kinzie) concluded not to give the whisky and arms to the savages. He did what any of us, common-sense, reasonable men, ignorant of the worst traits of the most cruel of races, might have done. He doubtless reasoned thus:

"I will destroy the means of frenzy and the implements of murder; then I will win the grateful allegiance of the Indian by magnificent gifts; stores that will make him rich beyond his wildest dream of comfort and abundance. Then I will throw myself and these defenceless ones on his protection."

Alas, he did not know with whom he was dealing! What is food and clothing to a devil demanding drink and gunpowder? He got only insolence in return for what he gave them, and loud curses for what he withheld. At the same time Mr. Kinzie could plainly see that if his whisky was destroyed by the government he might be reimbursed for it, while if it was left to the Indians the loss would be absolute and total.

Captain Heald held a council with the Indians on the afternoon of Wednesday, August 12, his juniors (according to Wau-Bun) declining his request to accompany him on the ground that they had secret information that the officers were to be massacred while in council; so he and Mr. Kinzie (interpreter) went boldly forth alone. When the two had walked out, the others opened the port-holes in the block-houses and trained the guns so as to command the assembly. No attack took place, and Captain Heald then promised the Indians a distribution of the goods—whether with or without any express reservations we do not know. The Indians, on their part, promised to escort the train in safety. (This would indicate that the promise was made to one tribe, the Pottowatomies, and that opposition might be looked for from another, probably the Winnebagoes.)

After the council, Mr. Kinzie had a long talk with Captain Heald, whereat it was agreed that all surplus arms, ammunition and liquor should not be distributed, but destroyed. This is Mrs. Kinzie's own account, and seems to set at rest the charge of bad faith (in not distributing all the goods) which has been made by Heald decryers and Indian apologists.

> On the thirteenth; the goods, consisting of blankets, broadcloths, calicoes, paints, etc., were distributed as stipulated. The same evening the ammunition and liquor were carried, part into the sally-port, and thrown into a well which had been dug there; the remainder was transported as secretly as possible through the northern gate, the heads of the barrels knocked in and the contents poured into the river. *The same fate was*

shared by a large quantity of alcohol belonging to Mr. Kinzie, which has, been deposited in a warehouse opposite the fort.[28]

The Indians suspected what was going on, and crept, serpent-like, as near the scene of action as possible, but a vigilant watch was kept up and no one was suffered to approach but those engaged in the affair. All the muskets not necessary for the command on the march were broken up and thrown in the well, together with bags of shot, flints, gun-screws and, in short, every weapon of offence. On the afternoon of the same day a second council was held with the Indians. They expressed great indignation at the destruction of the ammunition and liquor. Notwithstanding the precautions taken to preserve secrecy, the noise of knocking in the heads of the barrels had betrayed the operations, and so great was the quantity of liquor thrown into the river that the taste of the water next morning was, as one expressed it, "strong grog." (Wau-Bun narrative.)

William Wells, with the courage and endurance of his red foster-parents, and the faithful, loving heart of his own race, heard in some way (at Fort Wayne, where he was stationed) of the proposed evacuation of Fort Dearborn and the perilous flight to Detroit—nearly three hundred miles through the lonely "oak openings" of Michigan. His friends were here—his girl-friend, his own brother's daughter, Rebekah Wells Heald, was here. The thought of their danger summoned him like the sound of a trumpet to share it. He came at the head of a band of thirty Miami Indians, to guide, guard, help in every way the forlorn hope. It was too late to change the fatal plan, even if he would have tried to do so. He was a soldier, and obedience to orders was a part of his training. Besides, he knew the Indians, and they knew and respected him, and an expedition which would be desperate without his presence, might be changed by his help to a reasonable undertaking. If the whites had any friends among the reds, he would be at the head of those friends to lead them against the unfriendly.

---

[28] The italics are not used in the original. Mrs. Heald says that there was only one barrel of spirits in the fort.

How the hearts of the troubled little settlement must have bounded as they saw the help approaching! Fancy the scene!

On Friday, August 14th, when the sun was sinking in the West, there came along the lake-shore, stretched out beside the yellow sand-hills that extended southward clear down to the oak woods now marking the suburb of Hyde Park, the band of mounted Indians, headed by the good and brave soldier who knew the Indians as well as they knew each other. They had tramped all the way from Fort Wayne, one hundred and fifty miles, charged with the kindly, dangerous task of escorting the entire Chicago community back along the pathless forest they themselves had just come through.

Captain Heald unquestionably felt greatly reinvigorated, for this was an endorsement of his plan as well as help toward carrying it out. There could be no doubt at headquarters as to his coming, for here was an escorted officer arriving to bear him company. There was certainly a warm hand-shaking between the officers as they came together, and—one would like to have seen the meeting between uncle and niece! It was well neither could look forward twenty-four hours.

Even now the die was cast, and those behind the scenes knew that all was lost. Black Partridge, a chief friendly to the whites, had received, for services rendered at the time of the treaty of Greenville,[29] a silver medal bearing on one side a portrait of Madison, and on the other clasped hands, surmounted by tomahawk and "calumet," or pipe of peace, with the words "Peace and Friendship." Now he approached Captain Heald and delivered to him the significant emblem. His words, rendered by an interpreter, were these:

"Father, I come to deliver to you the medal I wear. It was given to me by the Americans, and I have long worn it in token of our mutual friendship. But our young men are resolved to imbue their hands in the blood of the whites. I cannot restrain them, and I will not wear a token of peace when I am compelled to act as an enemy." (Wau-Bun.)

---

[29] The treaty wherein the six miles square, which includes Chicago, was reserved to the whites.

Figure 15. Black Partridge Medal. From "Cyclopædia of United States History." Copyright, 1881, by Harper & Brothers.

This was equivalent to a declaration of hostilities, and a council of war, with Captain Wells as the most trusted adviser, would now have been most excellent. A plan of march should have been formed, including plan of battle, if battle should befall. Many advantages would be with the whites. For several days they would have the lake as their water supply and as a protection on one side. They had wagons to carry food, ammunition and the disabled, and to serve as a cover against musketry. They had between fifty and sixty armed and drilled regulars, twelve good militia-men and thirty Miamis, who could have been forced to fight if they had been properly held in hand—in all about one hundred men. They had a large supply of beef on the hoof, of which many, no doubt, were draught-oxen. On the whole, it is safe to say that, had they had a due sense of the condition of things, they might have made themselves, if not secure from attack, at least safe from annihilation; for, once massed behind the wagons, with the lake at their back, the first onslaught would have met such a rebuff as would have daunted the fickle Indian, who never perseveres against severe loss, no matter how great the stake or how heavy the damage he is inflicting on his enemy. One may now see how the defence should have been conducted when the fatal onslaught did occur. The wagons massed along the shore, the troops—regulars, militia and Miami escort, every man and woman who could fire or load a gun—using these wagons as a breastwork and defending them and the non-combatants crouching behind them; this would have discouraged the assailants and given time for a parley, during which the friendly Indians could have made their influence felt.

So easy it is to be wise after the event!

Mrs. Heald herself (through her son) gives us the following narrative:

> General Hull had sent orders to Captain Heald to evacuate the fort and come to Detroit, where he (Hull) was in command and preparing for a battle. The messenger arrived at Fort Dearborn about August 10. The evacuation took place August 15, 1812. The dispatch was brought by an Indian, and the date of the order showed that the fellow was a little too long in making the trip. He gave some excuse for this when the captain read the dispatch. He had gotten lame, or his moccasins had worn out, or something had occurred which made him a little late. But after Wells arrived—he came on the 12th or 13th, accompanied by thirty mounted Miamis—they talked the matter over and Wells said to Captain Heald: "Captain, that red rascal somehow or other was a longtime getting here. I fear he has notified the Indians along the way that the things will probably be distributed here and there may be considerable of a crowd. I don't fear anything serious, but I had much rather the Indian had come right straight here. He had no right to know, unless he was told, what the order was, but he got posted somehow as to what his business was about."
>
> At the time Wells arrived there were a few Indians there who had found out that the fort was to be vacated, and by the time they left there was a considerable party of them collected, all seemingly friendly with Captain Heald. Wells had very little idea there was to be a fight on the way, yet "smelt something in the air." But Captain Heald's orders were to vacate, and he must obey them unless something turned up that he could see was not right. They, however, discussed the probabilities of a siege. They had but few provisions, but little ammunition, and thought there was but little risk in going. Heald's orders were to dispose of things as he thought best. There was but little whisky. He thought what they had (one barrel) ought not to go into the hands of the Indians, nor should the munitions of war; and they took the whisky to a well that was inside the enclosure and poured it in, and what little arms and ammunition was left, besides what they took with them, was also thrown in.

John Kinzie, the trader at the post, objected to their going away, saying that his business would be interfered with—perhaps ruined. Captain Heald said he was sorry for that, but that he had to obey orders unless there was something objectionable to keep him from it. He advised Kinzie, however, not to allow the Indians to get to his alcohol, of which he had a considerable quantity—to pour it on the ground or in the river, or do something to dispose of it; that it would be unsafe, under the circumstances, to let the Indians have it. Mr. Kinzie suggested that the government might make this loss good, but this Captain Heald could not vouch for. The spirits were destroyed.

Suppose the veteran, Wells, tired with the tramping, the trifling and the turmoil, mounted on the roof of the block-house at the northwest corner of the stockade, and in the shadow of its motionless flag, pausing, and looking about him—what does he see?

Figure 16. William Wells.

A lonely, weedy streamlet flows eastward past the fort, then turns sharp to the right and makes its weak way by a shallow, fordable ripple, over a long sand-bar, into the lake, a half mile to the southward. At his feet, on the river bank, stands the United States Agency Storehouse. Across the river and a little to the eastward is the Kinzie house, built of squared logs by Jean Baptiste Pointe de Saible nearly forty years ago, now repaired, enlarged and improved by its owner and occupant, John Kinzie. A canoe lies moored to the bank in front of the house; when any of the numerous Kinzies wish to come to the fort they can paddle across; when any one wishes to go over he can halloo for the canoe. Just west of Kinzie's house is Ouillemette's cabin, and still further that of John Burns. Opposite Burns's place [near South State street] a swampy branch enters the river from the south, and on the sides of this branch there is a straggling lot of Indian wigwams—ominous sight! The north side of the river is all wooded, except where little garden-patches are cleared around the human habitations. The observer may see the forks of the stream a half-mile to the westward, but he cannot trace its branches, either "River Guarie," to the north, or "Portage River," to the south, for the trees hide them. Near him, to the west and south, sandy flats, grassy marshes and general desolation are all that he can see. (Will that barren waste ever be worth a dollar an acre?) Beyond, out of sight, past the bend of the South Branch, is Lee's place, with its fresh blood-stains and its two grassless graves.

Figure 17. Rebekah (Wells) Heald.

And so his eye wanders on, across the sandy flat, across the Indian trail, leading west of south, and the lake-shore trail which he himself came over, and finally rests with relief on the lake itself, the dancing blue water and the sky that covers it.

It is said that he who is about to die has sometimes a "second sight," a gift of looking forward to the days that are to follow his death.

Suppose the weary and anxious observer now to fall asleep, and in dreams to be gifted with this prophetic foresight, and to discern the change that four-score years are to bring.

It is 1892. Close at hand he sees the streamlet, now a mighty channel—a fine, broad, deep water-way, running straight between long piers out to the lake, and stretching » inland indefinitely; bordered by elephantine elevators, spanned by magnificent draw-bridges, each built of steel and moved by steam; carrying on its floods great propellers of 100,000 bushels of grain capacity. Looking north, west and south, he sees serried ranks of enormous buildings towering for miles on miles, each one so tall as to dwarf the fort and the block-house to nothingness. He sees hundreds of miles of paved streets, thronged with innumerable passengers and vehicles moving hither and thither, meeting and impeding each other, so that sometimes so many try to pass that none can pass; all must wait until the uniformed guardians of the peace bring order out of chaos. Every acre of ground in sight is worth millions of dollars.

His dreaming ears must be stunned by the thunder of commerce, his nostrils shocked by the smell of the vast food-factories, his skin smutched with the smoke of the burning fuel all about him, to keep these wheels in motion. Bewildered and dumbfounded, even more wearied than he had been by his waking view, he would fain turn his eyes to the east and rest them on the shining calm of the great lake, the dancing blue water and the sky that covers it.

And so we bid him good-bye. Whatever dream visited his tired soul that Friday night was his last. The next day was the one whereon his heroic death was to crown his brave, loving, faithful, fruitless effort to shield the innocent and helpless from a relentless doom.

As the fatal Saturday has been fully treated in Part First of this book, I now pass on to the dark days which followed it, and gather up the details, meager and scanty, of the later life of the survivors, and their death, so far known to the living world.

Chapter 5

FATE OF THE FUGITIVES

Every word bearing upon the adventures of the handful of Chicagoans left alive on Sunday, August 16th, 1812, has been carefully looked up and faithfully transcribed. Those words are few enough; the silence and darkness that enshroud their fate are more pathetically eloquent than speech could well be.

To begin with the Healds, who, as we have seen, were brought again together on the morning of August 16th, by the half-breed, Chandonnais. Darius Heald continues his report of his mother's narrative, as follows:

> It is thought that the Indians went off down the lake to have "a general frolic;" in other words, to torture to death the wounded prisoners. On the night of the sixteenth, Captain and Mrs. Heald, accompanied by an Indian named Robinson [probably Chief Robinson, well known in Chicago for many years], embarked in a canoe and, unmolested, commenced their journey to Mackinaw. Chandonnais' friendship was no half-way matter. They traveled all that night and all next day, until late in the evening, when they saw a young deer coming down to the water in a little clump of bushes to get a drink. They drew as near the shore as possible, and the Indian lad stepped out and waded to the shore, skipped down the bank behind the deer and shot it. Then they pitched camp, dressed the deer, using the hide as a kneading-board, whereon Mrs. Heald

stirred up some flour (they having brought a little in a leather bag from the fort) into a stiff paste, which she wound around sticks and toasted over the fire; and this Captain Heald afterward declared to be the finest bread he ever ate.

Here should come in, (according to Mrs. Helm's account in Wau-Bun) mention of a halt of some days at the mouth of the St. Joseph's river. It seems to me quite probable that the lapse of time had obliterated from Darius Heald's memory that part of his mother's narrative; or that he passed over, in talking to the stenographer, a matter which a timely question would have brought out. (See the Wau-Bun story, further on.)

They pushed on to Mackinaw, as Captain Heald said he had no chance of getting clear except by going to a British officer, and it was here that his parole was taken. It happened that Captain Heald and the officer in command at Mackinaw were both Free Masons, and Mrs. Heald says that they went off into a room by themselves, and that Captain Heald told his story and asked for help. He said that the Indians would pursue them, would not be more than twenty-four hours behind, and that a body would overtake them, and asked the British officer if he could protect them. The British officer said it would be a very hard matter in the fix they were in. If the Indians came down they might be overpowered; but that he would do this: He had a little "sailer" [a sailing-boat], and he would put Captain Heald and his wife in that and anchor it near the shore, and as soon as there were signs of Indians would signal them to start. He then took out his pocket-book and told Captain Heald to help himself "But," said Captain Heald, "we may never meet again." "That," said the officer, "makes no difference. You have a wife and I have no one on whom to spend money. I can do without it. You take it and use it, and if it is ever convenient to send it back you may do so." Mrs. Heald says she never knew why the officer should have been so kind to them, but laid it to the fact of their both being Masons; but said she "could never get anything out of him" (Captain Heald), although she tried more than once, and that she "never expected to get to know Masonic secrets."

However, Captain Heald did not take the money of the noble and generous enemy, for he had at that moment some two hundred dollars, probably in gold, which his provident wife had sewn in the cuffs of his undershirt, a circumstance which would indicate that she, at least, foresaw possible tribulation before they left the fort.

The Indians came in sight looking one hundred strong, and the British officer gave the sign for the little boat to move on. They went down to Detroit, and thence to Buffalo, whence they crossed to Pittsburg and went down the Ohio River, having procured, through an officer, some conveyance by which to go down the river, and they then drifted down, part of the way by boat and part of the way by raft, and in this way reached Kentucky soil. They reached Mrs. Heald's old home by night, past midnight, and rapped for admittance. Colonel Samuel Wells asked, "Who's there?" "A friend," said Captain Heald. "Well, who are you?" "Well, I am a friend." Mrs. Heald then spoke up and said, "Yes, two friends." Colonel Wells thought he recognized a woman's voice, and came to the door and opened it, and found himself face to face with his daughter, whom he had not seen for nearly two years, whom he had supposed to be dead, who left him as a bride and returned home as a wounded prisoner. They had been two months on the way from Fort Dearborn to Kentucky.

Before her death, in 1856, Mrs. Heald had dictated to Mrs. Kerr, her niece, a large number of facts connected with her life. The manuscript was foolscap, and contained, Mr. Heald thinks, some hundreds of pages. It was in existence up to the time of the Union War, and he remembers seeing it wrapped up in a newspaper and tied with twine, at the Heald residence, in St. Charles County, Missouri, near the town of O'Fallon. During one of the incursions of Union soldiers the house was ransacked from top to bottom. Captain Heald's sword was taken away, and, greatest loss of all, that manuscript then disappeared, Mr. Heald thinks probably destroyed—burned among other papers supposed to be of no value.

A negro boy, who had been raised by Mr. Heald, received word that that sword had been left somewhere not far from home, and was then being used as a corn-knife, and he obtained it and brought it back to Mr. Heald, who recognized it as what was left of his father's old sword; but alas! the manuscript has never been heard of—probably never will be. This is the nearest approach now possible to a reproduction of the facts it contained.

The Wau-Bun narrative is more circumstantial, if not more trustworthy, and tends naturally in a different direction. It goes on:

> Along with Mr. Kinzie's party was a non-commissioned officer who had made his escape in a singular manner. As the troops were about leaving the fort it was found that the baggage horses of the surgeon had strayed off. The quartermaster-sergeant, Griffith, was sent to collect them and bring them on, it being absolutely necessary to recover them, since their packs contained part of the surgeon's apparatus and the medicines for the march.
>
> This man had been for a long time on the sick report, and for this reason was given the charge of the baggage instead of being placed with the troops. His efforts to recover the horses being unsuccessful, he was hastening to rejoin his party, alarmed at some appearances of disorder and hostile indications among the Indians, when he was met and made prisoner by To-pee-nee-be.
>
> Having taken from him his arms and accoutrements, the chief put him in a canoe and paddled him across the river, bidding him make for the woods and secrete himself. This he did, and the following day in the afternoon, seeing from his lurking-place that all appeared quiet, he ventured to steal cautiously into the garden of Ouilmette, where he concealed himself for a time behind some currant-bushes.
>
> At length he determined to enter the house, and accordingly climbed up through a small back window into the room where the family were. This was just as the Wabash Indians left the house of Ouilmette for that of Mr. Kinzie. The danger of the sergeant was now imminent. The family stripped him of his uniform and arrayed him in a suit of deerskin, with belt, moccasins and pipe, like a French engage. His dark complexion and large black whiskers favored the disguise. The family were all ordered to address him in French, and although utterly ignorant of the language, he continued to pass for a Weem-tee-gosh,[30] and as such to accompany Mr. Kinzie and his family, undetected by his enemies, until they reached a place of safety.
>
> On the third day after the battle, the family of Mr. Kinzie, with the clerks of the establishment, were put into a boat under the care of

---

[30] Frenchman.

François, a half-breed interpreter, and conveyed to St. Joseph's, where they remained until the following November, under the protection of To-pe-nee-bee's band. They were then conducted to Detroit under the escort of Chandonnais and their trusty Indian friend, Kee-po-tah, and delivered up as prisoners of war to Colonel McKee, the British Indian Agent.

Mr. Kinzie was not allowed to leave St. Joseph's with his family, his Indian friends insisting on his remaining and endeavoring to secure some remnant of his scattered property. During his excursions with them for that purpose he wore the costume and paint of the tribe, in order to escape capture and perhaps death at the hands of those who were still thirsting for blood. In time, however, his anxiety for his family induced him to follow them to Detroit, where in the month of January he was received and paroled by General Proctor.

Captain and Mrs. Heald had been sent across the lake to St. Joseph's, the day after the battle. The former had received two wounds and the latter seven in the engagement.

Figure 18. Alexander Robinson (in old age). Chief of the Pottowatomies, Chippewas, and others.

Lieutenant Helm, who was likewise wounded, was carried by some friendly Indian to their village on the Au Sable, and thence to Peoria, where he was liberated by the intervention of Mr. Thomas Forsyth, the half-brother of Mr. Kinzie. Mrs. Helm had accompanied her parents to St.

Joseph's, where they resided in the family of Alexander Robinson,[31] receiving from them all possible kindness and hospitality for several months.

After their arrival in Detroit Mrs. Helm was joined by her husband, when they were both arrested, by order of the British commander, and sent on horseback, in the dead of winter, through Canada, to Fort George, on the Niagara frontier. When they arrived at that post there seemed no official appointed to receive them, and notwithstanding their long and fatiguing journey, in weather the most cold and inclement, Mrs. Helm, a delicate woman of seventeen years, was permitted to sit waiting in her saddle, without the gate, for more than an hour before the refreshment of fire or food, or even the shelter of a roof, was offered to her. When Colonel Sheaffe, who had been absent at the time, was informed of this brutal inhospitality, he expressed the greatest indignation. He waited on Mrs. Helm immediately, apologized in the most courteous manner, and treated her and Lieutenant H. with the most considerate kindness, until, by an exchange of prisoners, they were liberated and found means to reach their friends in Steuben County, New York.

Captain Heald had been taken prisoner by an Indian from the Kankakee who had a strong personal regard for him, and who, when he saw the wounded and enfeebled state of Mrs. H., released her husband that he might accompany his wife to St. Joseph's. To the latter place they were accordingly carried, as has been related, by Chandonnais and his party. In the meantime, the Indian who had so nobly released his prisoner returned to his village on the Kankakee, where he had the mortification of finding that his conduct had excited great dissatisfaction among his band. So great was the displeasure manifested that he resolved to make a journey to St. Joseph's and reclaim his prisoner. News of his intention being brought to To-pee-nee-bee and Kee-po-tah, under whose care the prisoners were, they held a private council with Chandonnais, Mr. Kinzie and the principal men of the village, the result of which was, a determination to send Captain and Mrs. Heald to the island of Mackinac and deliver them up to the British. They were accordingly put in a bark canoe and paddled by Robinson and his wife a distance of three hundred

---

[31] This Pottowatomie chief, well known to many of the citizens of Chicago, was residing at Aux Plaines when Wau-Bun was written.

miles along the coast of Michigan, and surrendered as prisoners of war to the commanding officer at Mackinac.

This, though discordant with the shorter report received from the Healds, certainly seems to have sound basis of truth. I have no doubt that the Captain and his wife did halt at St. Joseph's and that John Kinzie had something to do with their further journey to Mackinac. Wau-Bun proceeds:

> As an instance of the procrastinating spirit of Captain Heald it may be mentioned that even after he had received certain intelligence that his Indian captor was on his way from the Kankakee to St. Joseph's to retake him, he would still have delayed another day at that place to make preparation for a more comfortable journey to Mackinac.

Mrs. Helm's acuteness in finding flaws in Captain Heald is quite interesting. But as this Kankakee information must have come entirely through Indian channels, and as the savage plan is ever to strike first and warn afterward, I am prone to suspect that he applied the "personal equation," and made light of the tale; and that there was in fact little in it to frighten a brave man and his heroic wife. (*Per contra*, see the Mackinaw incident.)

> The soldiers, with their wives and surviving children, were dispersed among the different villages of the Pottowatomies, upon the Illinois, Wabash and Rock River, and at Milwaukee, until the following spring, when they were, for the most part, carried to Detroit and ransomed.

We should like to believe the hopeful views here given regarding the fate of the remaining prisoners. In truth, this account is as well authenticated as is that given in the Niles' Register, as copied from a Plattsburgh (N. Y.) newspaper, and given later in this work.

> Mrs. Burns, with her infant, became the prisoners of a chief who carried her to his village and treated her with great kindness. His wife,

from jealousy of the favor shown to the white woman and her child, always treated them with great hostility. On one occasion she struck the infant with a tomahawk, and narrowly missed her aim of putting an end to it altogether.[32] They were not long left in the power of the old hag, after this demonstration, but on the first opportunity carried to a place of safety.

The family of Mr. Lee had resided in a house on the lake-shore, not far from the fort. Mr. Lee was the owner of Lee's Place, which he cultivated as a farm. It was his son who ran down with a discharged soldier to give the alarm of "Indians" at the fort on the afternoon of the 7th of April. The father, the son, and all the other members had fallen victims on the 15th of August, except Mrs. Lee and her young infant. These were claimed by Black Partridge and carried to his village on the Au Sable. He had been particularly attached to a little girl of Mrs. Lee's, about twelve years of age. This child had been placed on horseback for the march, and as she was unaccustomed to the exercise, she was tied fast to the saddle, lest by any accident she should slip off or be thrown.

She was within reach of the balls at the commencement of the engagement, and was severely wounded. The horse set off on a full gallop, which partly threw her, but she was held fast by the bands which confined her, and hung dangling as the animal ran violently about. In this state she was met by Black Partridge, who caught the horse and disengaged her from the saddle. Finding her so much wounded that she could not recover, and that she was suffering great agony, he put the finishing stroke to her at once with his tomahawk. He afterwards said that this was the hardest thing he ever tried to do, but he did it because he could not bear to see her suffer.

He took the mother and her infant to his village, where he became warmly attached to the former—so much so that he wished to marry her; but, as she very naturally objected, he treated her with the greatest respect and consideration. He was in no hurry to release her, for he was in hopes of prevailing on her to become his wife. In the course of the winter her child fell ill. Finding that none of the remedies within their reach were effectual, Black Partridge proposed to take the little one to Chicago,

---

[32] Twenty-two years after this, as I was on a journey to Chicago in the steamer Uncle Sam, a young woman, hearing my name, introduced herself to me, and raising her hair from her forehead, showed me the mark of the tomahawk which had so nearly been fatal to her. (Mrs. Kinzie, in Wau-Bun.)

where there was now a French trader living in the mansion of Mr. Kinzie, and procure some medical aid from him. Wrapping up his charge with the greatest care he set out on his journey.

When he arrived at the residence of M. du Pin, he entered the room where he was, and carefully placed his burden on the floor.

"What have you there?" asked M. du Pin.

"A young raccoon which I brought you as a present," was the reply, and opening the pack he showed the little sick infant.

When the trader had prescribed for its complaint, and Black Partridge was about to return to his home, he told his friend his proposal to Mrs. Lee to become his wife, and the manner in which it had been received.

M. du Pin entertained some fears that the chiefs resolution might not hold out, to leave it to the lady herself whether to receive his addresses or not, so he entered at once into a negotiation for her ransom, and so effectually wrought upon the good feelings of Black Partridge that he consented to bring his fair prisoner at once to Chicago, that she might be restored to her friends.

Whether the kind trader had at the outset any other feeling than sympathy and brotherly kindness, we cannot say—we only know that in process of time, Mrs. Lee became Madame du Pin, and that they lived together in great happiness for many years after.

So disappears, from earliest Chicago annals, the name of Lee. The father had been a householder, living somewhere about where the new Public Library is now building, and his farm was (after Père Marquette's "cabinage") the very first settlement on the West Side of the South Branch or "Portage River." His son escaped from the murderers at "Hardscrabble" in spring, only to perish, with his father, during the massacre, or perhaps in the "general frolic" that followed. Then the widow becomes Mrs. du Pin and we hear no more of the Lees. There is a grim completeness about the domestic drama. On Friday it has father, mother, son, daughter and baby, on Saturday, father and son are killed in battle (or by torture) and daughter mangled by a horse's feet and finished by a tomahawk; a few months later the puny baby is brought in to be "doctored" and then the widow marries again and lives on "in great happiness."

The fate of Nau-non-gee, one of the chiefs of the Calumet village, and who is mentioned in the early part of the narrative, deserves to be recorded.

During the battle of the 15th of August, the chief object of his attack was one Sergeant Hays, a man from whom he had received many acts of kindness.

After Hays had received a ball through the body, this Indian ran up to tomahawk him, when the Sergeant, collecting his remaining strength, pierced him through the body with his bayonet. They fell together. Other Indians running up soon dispatched Hays, and it was not until then that his bayonet was extracted from the body of his adversary.

The wounded chief was carried after the battle to his village on the Calumet, where he survived for several days. Finding his end approaching; he called together his young men, and enjoined them in the most solemn manner to regard the safety of their prisoners after his death, and to take the lives of none of them, from respect to his memory, as he deserved his fate from the hands of those whose kindness he had so ill-requited.

Figure 19. Tecumseh. From "Cyclopædia of United States History."—Copyright, 1881, by Harper & Brothers.

Chapter 6

JOHN KINZIE'S CAPTIVITY

We are, and always were (and I hope always will be), anything but a "military nation." 1813 opened very gloomily for the United States; but, as our quiet country has shown in several times of trial, it takes some disaster to wake up Americans to the claims of the land they love and the government they themselves have made. Bunker Hill was a defeat, in form, but the patriots only fell back a little way; then halted and quietly remarked: "We have several more hills to sell at the same price," the price being such a loss as the British army had rarely met. The war of 1812 began with the loss of Mackinaw and Detroit on land and the frigate Chesapeake at sea; but Scott at Chippewa and Lundy's Lane, Harrison at the Thames and Jackson at New Orleans caused all land reverses to be forgotten; while Perry's victory on Lake Erie, together with a splendid cluster of triumphs on the ocean, gave our navy a lustre which it has never lost or suffered to become tarnished.

Curiously enough, Mr. Kinzie, our own Chicago pioneer, was a witness to the finish of the glorious day at Put-in-bay, in announcing which Commodore Oliver Hazard Perry added to our war-cries the immortal words, "We have met the enemy and they are ours."

Here is Mrs. Kinzie's narrative of the captivity of her father-in-law, embodying his experiences at that time:

Captivity of John Kinzie

It had been a stipulation of General Hull at the surrender of Detroit that the inhabitants of that place should remain undisturbed in their homes. Accordingly the family of Mr. Kinzie took up their quarters with their friends in the old mansion which many will still recall as standing on the northeast corner of Jefferson Avenue and Wayne Street.

The feelings of indignation and sympathy were constantly aroused in the hearts of the citizens during the winter that ensued. They were almost daily called upon to witness the cruelties practiced upon American prisoners brought in by their Indian captors. Those who could scarcely drag their wounded, bleeding feet over the frozen ground, were compelled to dance for the amusement of the savages, and these exhibitions sometimes took place before the government house, the residence of Colonel McKee. Some of the British officers looked down from their windows at these heart-rending performances; for the honor of humanity we will hope such instances were rare.

Everything that could be made available among the effects of the citizens were offered, to ransom their countrymen from the hands of these inhuman beings. The prisoners brought in from the River Raisin—those unfortunate men who were permitted, after their surrender to General Proctor, to be tortured and murdered by inches by his savage allies, excited the sympathies and called for the action of the whole community. Private houses were turned into hospitals, and everyone was forward to get possession of as many as possible of the survivors. To effect this even the articles of their apparel were bartered by the ladies of Detroit, as they watched from their doors or windows the miserable victims being carried about for sale.

In the dwelling of Mr. Kinzie, one large room was devoted to the reception of these sufferers. Few of them survived. Among those spoken of as the objects of deepest interest, were two young gentlemen of Kentucky, both severely wounded, and their wounds aggravated to a mortal degree by subsequent ill-usage and hardships. Their solicitude for each other and their exhibition in various ways of the most tender fraternal affection created an impression never to be forgotten.

The last bargain made was by Black Jim, and one of the children, who had permission to redeem a negro servant of the gallant Colonel

Allen, with an old white horse, the only available article that remained among their possessions.

A brother of Colonel Allen afterward came to Detroit, and the negro preferred returning to servitude rather than remaining a stranger in a strange land.

Mr. Kinzie, as has been related, joined his family at Detroit in the month of January. A short time after, suspicions arose that he was in correspondence with General Harrison, who was now at Fort Meigs, and who was believed to be meditating an advance upon Detroit. Lieutenant Watson of the British army waited upon Mr. Kinzie one day with an invitation to the quarters of General Proctor on the opposite side of the river, saying he wished to speak with him on business. Quite unsuspicious, he complied with the invitation, when to his surprise he was ordered into confinement, and strictly guarded in the house of his former partner, Mr. Patterson of Sandwich. Finding he did not return to his home, Mrs. Kinzie informed some of the Indian chiefs, his particular friends, who immediately repaired to the headquarters of the commanding officer, demanded their "friend's" release and brought him back to his home. After awaiting a time until a favorable opportunity presented itself, the General sent a detachment of dragoons to arrest him. They had succeeded in carrying him away and crossing the river with him. Just at this moment a party of friendly Indians made their appearance.

"Where is Shaw-nee-aw-kee?" was the first question.

"There," replied his wife, pointing across the river, "in the hands of the red-coats who are taking him away again."

The Indians ran to the river, seized some canoes that they found there, and crossing over to Sandwich compelled General Proctor a second time to forego his intentions.

A third time this officer was more successful, and succeeded in arresting Mr. Kinzie and conveying him, heavily ironed, to Fort Maiden in Canada, at the mouth of the Detroit river. Here he was at first treated with great severity, but after a time the rigor of his confinement was somewhat relaxed, and he was permitted to walk on the bank of the river for air and exercise.

On the 10th of September, as he was taking his promenade under the close supervision of a guard of soldiers, the whole party were startled by the sound of guns on Lake Erie at no great distance below. What could it mean? It must be Commodore Barclay firing into some of the Yankees. The firing continued. The time allotted the prisoner for his daily walk expired, but neither he nor his guard observed the lapse of time, so anxiously were they listening to what they now felt sure was an engagement between ships of war. At length Mr. Kinzie was reminded that the hour for his return to confinement had arrived. He petitioned for another half hour.

"Let me stay," said he, "until we can learn how the battle has gone."

Very soon a sloop appeared under press of sail, rounding the point, and, presently, two gun-boats in chase of her.

"She is running—she bears the British colors," cried he—"yes, yes, they are lowering. She is striking her flag! Now," turning to the soldiers, "I will go back to prison contented, I know how the battle has gone."

The sloop was the Little Belt, the last of the squadron captured by the gallant Perry, on that memorable occasion, which he announced in the immortal words: "We have met the enemy and they are ours!"

Matters were growing critical, and it was necessary to transfer all prisoners to a place of greater security than the frontier was now likely to be. It was resolved therefore to send Mr. Kinzie to the mother country. Nothing has ever appeared which would explain this course of General Proctor in regard to this gentleman. He had been taken from the bosom of his family, where he was living quietly under the parole which he had received, and was protected by the stipulations of the surrender. He was kept for months in confinement. Now he was placed on horseback under a strong guard, who announced that they had orders to shoot him through the head if he offered to speak to a person on the road. He was tied upon the saddle in a way to prevent his escape, and thus they set out for Quebec. A little incident occurred which will help to illustrate the course invariably pursued toward our citizens at this period, by the British army on the northwestern frontier.

The saddle upon which Mr. Kinzie rode had not been properly fastened, and owing to the rough motion of the animal on which it was, it turned so as to bring the rider into a most awkward and painful position. His limbs being fastened he could not disengage himself, and in this manner he was compelled by those who had charge of him, to ride until he was nearly exhausted, before they had the humanity to release him.

John Kinzie's Captivity

Figure 20. New Fort, River, Kinzie House, Etc., as Given in Wau-Bun.

Arrived at Quebec, he was put on board a small vessel to be sent to England. The vessel when a few days out at sea was chased by an American frigate and driven into Halifax. A second time she set sail when she sprang a leak and was compelled to put back.

The attempt to send him across the ocean was now abandoned, and he was returned to Quebec. Another step, equally inexplicable with his arrest, was now taken. This was his release, and that of Mr. Macomb, of Detroit, who was also in confinement at Quebec, and the permission given them to return to their friends and families, although the war was not yet ended. It may possibly be imagined that in the treatment these gentlemen received, the British commander sheltered himself under the plea of their being "native born British subjects," and perhaps when it was ascertained that Mr. Kinzie was indeed a citizen of the United States, it was thought safest to release him.

In the meantime General Harrison at the head of his troops had reached Detroit. He landed on the 29th of September. All the citizens went forth to meet him.—Mrs. Kinzie leading her children by the hand, was of the number. The General accompanied her to her home and took up his abode there. On his arrival he was introduced to Kee-po-tah, who happened to be on a visit to the family at that time. The General had seen the chief the preceding year, at the council at Vincennes, and the meeting was one of great cordiality and interest.

Additional particulars about the interesting career of this remarkable man are given further on. (See Appendix D.)

Chapter 7

CONTEMPORANEOUS REPORTS

Figure 21. Massacre Tree, 18th Street.

Hardly any one institution existing four score years ago, shows so wondrous a change as does the American newspaper. The steamboat, railroad, telegraph, telephone, power-press and other mechanical aids to the spreading of news have all been invented and perfected within that time, while gas and electric light have aided in the prompt reproduction of intelligence, and penny-postage in its dissemination. So that which was then an infant—say rather an embryo—is now a giant.

The very first published narrative of the massacre which is now at hand is the following account, very short and full of errors, taken from the Buffalo Gazette (date not given) and published in Niles' Weekly Register of October 3, 1812.[33]

> *Fall of Fort Dearborn, at Chicago.*—Yesterday afternoon the Queen Charlotte arrived at Fort Erie, seven days from Detroit. A flag of truce soon landed, at Buffalo Creek, Major Atwater and Lieut. J. L. Eastman, who gave the following account of the fall of Fort Dearborn: On the first of September a Pottowatomie chief arrived at Detroit and stated that about the middle of August Captain Wells, from Fort Wayne [an interpreter], arrived at Fort Dearborn to advise the commandant of that fort to evacuate it and retreat. In the meantime a large body of Indians of different nations had collected and menaced the garrison. A council was held with the Indians, in which it was agreed that the party in the garrison should be spared on condition that all property in the fort should be given up. The Americans marched out but were fired upon and nearly all killed. There were about fifty men in the fort beside women and children, and probably not more than ten or twelve taken prisoners. Captain Wells and Heald [the commandant] were killed.

This brief report interests us in various ways. Detroit was in the British hands, and the Queen Charlotte a British ship, for Perry's victory had not yet been won. Major Atwater and Lieut. Eastman, here liberated by the British under flag of truce, were probably part of the army surrendered by General Hull on August 16, and paroled; these officers having remained in

---

[33] This paper, published in Baltimore, was the best general chronicle of events reported by correspondents or appearing in the few and meager outlying journals of the day.

Detroit for some unexplained reason—perhaps because they were citizens of that city, as Atwater is an old Detroit name. (It has been given to a street there.) The Queen Charlotte was one of the ships captured by Perry on Sept. 10, 1813, and was sunk in Put-in-Bay, and twenty years later she was raised, repaired and put again in commission, this time as a trading-vessel, and it was on her that John Dean Caton, later Chief Justice of Illinois, and now (1893) an honored resident of Chicago, took passage at Buffalo with his bride, in 1834, and came to the land which was to be their home for sixty years.[34]

Regarding the rest of the fugitives we have very scanty reports. The next item we find is an utterly wild, false and fanciful statement of Mrs. Helm's vicissitudes, contradicting in every particular her own narrative, as given in Wau-Bun.

> [From Niles' Weekly Register, Saturday, April 13, 1813.]
>
> *Savage Barbarity.*—Mrs. Helm, the wife of Lieutenant Helm, who escaped from the butchery of Chicauga by the assistance of a humane Indian, has arrived at this place [Buffaloe]. The account of her sufferings during three months' slavery among the Indians and three months' imprisonment among their allies, would make a most interesting volume. One circumstance alone will I mention. During five days after she was taken prisoner she had not the least sustenance, and was compelled to drag a canoe (barefooted and wading along the stream) in which there were some squaws, and when she demanded food, some flesh of her murdered countrymen and a piece of Col. Wells' heart was offered her.
>
> She knows the fact that Col. Proctor, the British commander at Maiden, bought the scalps of our murdered garrison of Chicauga, and thanks to her noble spirit, she boldly charged him with his infamy in his own house.
>
> She knows further, from the tribe with whom she was a prisoner, and who were the perpetrators of those murders, that they intended to remain true, but that they received orders from the British to cut off our garrison, whom they were to escort.

---

[34] Mrs. Caton died in 1892.

Oh, spirits of the murdered Americans! can ye not rouse your countrymen, your friends, your relations, to take ample vengeance on those worse than savage bloodhounds?
An Officer.
March 18th, 1813.

This is manifestly written to "fire the patriotic heart" of the country to rally to the defence of "Buffaloe," a frontier town in deadly fear of its Canadian neighbors, in sight beyond the Niagara River. Mrs. Helm herself must have learned with surprise that while she, with the rest of the Kinzie family, was hospitably entertained at "Parc-aux-vaches," on the St. Joseph, she was suffering "three months' slavery among the Indians;" and later, while living in Detroit, she was enduring "three months' imprisonment among their allies," the English. Also that during the five days after the massacre, when she tells us she was, with much discomfort and more alarm, living in the Kinzie mansion with her relatives, she was really dragging a canoe, barefooted, wading along the stream, deprived of all sustenance except the flesh of her murdered countrymen, especially poor Wells's carved-up and bleeding heart—which, by the way, she had only heard of; never seen! Such things serve very well to prove to us that, as creators of imaginative fiction, newspaper correspondents of those days were equal even to those of our own.

More absurd, if possible, is a letter printed in Niles' Register of May 8, 1813, purporting to have been written by one Walter Jordan, a non-commissioned officer of regulars, stationed at Fort Wayne, to his wife, in Alleghany County, dated Fort Wayne, October 19, 1812. In the first place, it is most unlikely that any such white man should have been in Captain Wells's company and remained unmentioned. We hear of nobody as arriving but Captain Wells and his thirty Miami Indians. In our day, it is true, a captain would be likely to be accompanied by an orderly; but Wells had been brought up in too stern a school to be provided with such an attendant. Then, too, the narrative bristles with absurdities. The story is as follows:

I take my pen to inform you that I am well, after a long and perilous journey through the Indian country. Capt. Wells, myself, and an hundred friendly Indians, left Fort Wayne on the 1st of August to escort Captain Heald from Fort Chicauga, as he was in danger of being captured by the British. Orders had been given to abandon the fort and retreat to Fort Wayne, a distance of 150 miles. We reached Chicauga on the 10th of August, and on the 15th prepared for an immediate march, burning all that we could not fetch with us. On the 15th at 8 o'clock we commenced our march with our small force, which consisted of Captain Wells, myself, one hundred Confute Indians, Captain Heald's one hundred men, ten women, twenty children—in all 232. We had marched half a mile when we were attacked by 600 Kickapoo and Wynbago Indians. In the moment of trial our Confute savages joined the savage enemy. Our contest lasted fifteen minutes, when every man, woman and child was killed except fifteen. Thanks be to God, I was one of those who escaped. First they shot the feather off my cap, next the epaulet off my shoulder, and then the handle from the sword; I then surrendered to four savage rascals. The Confute chief, taking me by the hand and speaking English, said: "Jordan, I know you. You gave me tobacco at Fort Wayne. We won't kill you, but come and see what we will do to your captain." So, leading me to where Wells lay, they cut off his head and put it on a long pole, while another took out his heart and divided it up among the chiefs and ate it up raw. Then they scalped the slain and stripped the prisoners, and gathered in a ring with us fifteen poor wretches in the middle. They had nearly fallen out about the divide, but my old chief, the White Racoon, holding me fast, they made the divide and departed to their towns. They tied me hard and fast that night, and placed a guard over me. I lay down and slept soundly until morning, for I was tired. In the morning they untied me and set me parching corn, at which I worked attentively until night. They said that if I would stay, and not run away they would make a chief of me; but if I would attempt to run away they would catch me and burn me alive. I answered them with a fine story in order to gain their confidence, and finally made my escape from them on the 19th of August, and took one of the best horses to carry me, being seven days in the wilderness. I was joyfully received at Wayne on the 26th. On the 28th day they attacked the fort and blockaded us until the 16th of September, when we were relieved by General Harrison.

One is uncertain whether to rate this as a yarn made by some penny-a-liner out of such scraps as might be picked up from common rumor and the tales of returned stragglers of the thirty Indians who ran away when the attack began, or the lying story of a fellow who was really of the party, and one of the leaders, not in the fight, but in the flight. His enumeration of "one hundred Confute Indians," (no tribe of that name being known to history) in place of the band of thirty Miamis, his estimate of Captain Heald's "one hundred men, ten women and twenty children," his march of "half a mile," his statement that all were killed except fifteen, which would make the loss of life over two hundred, in place of Captain Heald's estimate of fifty-two, all tend to force the conclusion that there was no Walter Jordan in the matter. The latter part of the story, representing himself as heroically losing feather, epaulet and sword-hilt to the rascally savages, who still refrained from inflicting bodily injury on him, his then being kindly but firmly led to the place where poor Wells, in the presence of his niece, was waiting to have his head cut off and set up on a pole, and his heart cut out and divided among the chiefs, etc., tends to the belief that Walter Jordan was present, ran away, saved himself, reached Fort Wayne and devised this cock-and-bull story to explain his long absence, his personal safety and his possession of a horse which did not belong to him. Another hypothesis is that he started from Fort Wayne with Wells, deserted on the road, hung around until he got the story as told by the Indian fugitives, and (finding that his captain was dead) put a bold face on the matter and came in, bringing a horse he had been lucky enough to "capture" when its owner was not looking.

The next item is dated more than a year later; a year during which the wretched captives seem to have suffered miseries indescribable. The story bears the stamp of truth so far as the escaped fugitives knew it:

[From Niles' Weekly Register, 4th June, 1814.]
Chicago.—Among the persons who have recently arrived at this place, says the Plattsburg [N. Y.] paper of the 21st ultimo, from Quebec, are: James Van Horn, Dyson Dyer, Joseph Knowles, Joseph Bowen, Paul Grummond, Nathan Edson, Elias Mills, James Corbin, Phelim Corbin, of the First Regiment of U. S. Infantry, who survived the massacre at Fort

Dearborn, or Chicago, on the 15th August, 1812. It will be recollected that the commandant at Fort Chicago, Captain Heald, was ordered by General Hull to evacuate the fort and proceed with his command to Detroit; that having proceeded about a mile and a half, the troops were attacked by a body of Indians, to whom they were compelled to capitulate.

Captain Heald, in his report of this affair, dated October 23d, 1812, says: "Our strength was fifty-four regulars and twelve militia, out of which twenty-six regulars and all the militia, with two women and twelve children, were killed in the action.

"Lieut. Linai T. Helm, with twenty-five non-commissioned officers and privates, and eleven women and children, were prisoners when we separated." Lieut. Helm was ransomed. Of the twenty-five non-commissioned officers and privates, and the eleven women and children, the nine persons above mentioned are believed to be the only survivors. They state that the prisoners who were not put to death on the march were taken to the Fox River, in the Indian territory, where they were distributed among the Indians as servants. Those who survived remained in this situation about nine months, during which time they were allowed scarcely a sufficiency of sustenance to support nature, and were then brought to Fort Chicago, where they were purchased by a French trader, agreeable to the directions of General Proctor, and sent to Amherstburg, and from thence to Quebec, where they arrived November 8th, 1813.

John Neads, who was one of the prisoners, formerly of Virginia, died among the Indians between the 15th and 20th of January, 1813.

Hugh Logan, an Irishman, was tomahawked and put to death, be not being able to walk from excessive fatigue.

August Mott, a German, was killed in the same manner for the like reason.

A man by the name of Nelson was frozen to death while a captive with the Indians. He was formerly from Maryland.

A child of Mrs. Neads, the wife of John Neads, was tied to a tree to prevent its following and crying after its mother for victuals. Mrs.. Neads perished from hunger and cold.

The officers who were killed on the 15th of August had their heads cut off and their hearts taken out and boiled in the presence of the prisoners. Eleven children were massacred and scalped in one wagon.

Mrs. Corbin, wife of Phelim Corbin, in an advanced stage of pregnancy, was tomahawked, scalped, cut open, and had the child taken out and its head cut off.

Turning to the latest muster-roll of the force, dated 1810, we identify among these survivors the names of Dyson Dyer, Nathan Edson, Paul Grummow, James Van Home, James Corbin and Phelim Corbin. Among the perished, August Mott, John Neads and Hugh Logan. To this sad list must be added four still more pitiable victims—the wife and unborn child of Phelim Corbin, and the unhappy Mrs. Neads, to whom death must have been welcome after seeing her little one "tied to a tree to keep it from following her and crying for victuals."

Figure 22. The Second Block-House in Its Last Days.

Mrs. John Kinzie, in a sketch of the life of her husband (Chic. Hist. Society, July 11, 1877. Fergus' Hist. Series No. 10) says:

In 1816 the Kinzie family returned to their desolated home in Chicago. The bones of the murdered soldiers, who had fallen four years before, were still lying unburied where they had fallen. The troops who rebuilt the fort collected and interred these remains. The coffins which contained them were deposited near the bank of the river, which then had its outlet about at the foot of Madison Street. The cutting through the sand-bar for the harbor caused the lake to encroach and wash away the earth, exposing the long range of coffins and their contents, which were afterward cared for and reinterred by the civil authorities.

There is good reason to believe that Mrs. Kinzie was mistaken in thinking that the coffins exposed on the lake shore by the action of the waves, contained the bodies of those who perished in the massacre. The fort burying-ground certainly was at the place indicated, and the exposed coffins doubtless contained the bodies of those buried in that ground; but that does not include the massacre victims. Mr. Fernando Jones believes them to have been buried at where Seventeenth Street, extended, would cross Prairie Avenue.

A letter on the matter (kindly furnished me while these pages are in preparation) reads as follows:

> Upon my arrival in Chicago, in the spring of 1835, being fifteen years of age, I became acquainted with a number of Indian and half-breed boys, as well as older persons, and visited many times the location of the Indian massacre of 1812. The spot was pointed out by some who were children at the time, and by others who had been informed by their parents. The burial-place where the victims were interred was quite distinct at that time. There was a mound in the prairie southwest of the massacre-ground, that was pointed out as the grave of the vidette, or soldier in advance of the retreating garrison.
>
> The tradition was that the soldier ran west into the prairie, thinking to hide in the tall grass, but was pursued and killed and scalped and his body afterward buried by friendly half breeds.
>
> In the summer of 1836 a number of youngsters, accompanied by some young Indians and half-breeds, proceeded to examine the lonely hillock in the plains. The turf still preserved the shape of a grave. There were in the party as I remember, besides myself, Pierre Laframbois, Alex Beaubien, Charles Cleaver, J. Louis Hooker and John C. Haines. After

digging about three feet into the ground we unearthed a skeleton surrounded by bits of woolen cloth, pieces of leather, brass military buttons and buckles and a brass plate with U. S. upon it. We became convinced that this was undeniably the grave of the traditional vidette, and reverently returned the remains into the grave where they had lain for a quarter of a century, and where I suppose they still remain. The spot was about a block south of the Calumet Club-House, near the S. E. corner of Indiana Ave. and Twenty-first Street. I kept watch of the place until streets were laid out and the property improved, having resided near it for over twenty-five years.

FERNANDO JONES

No remains of any coffin were found, a fact which would indicate a battle-field burial; but on the other hand, it seems most improbable that the Indians would have left belt-plate, buttons and cloth on any of their victims.

The Indian Problem is solved at last, and by the Indians' own and only means for the solution of problems—the cutting of the knot. It has been a long struggle, marked by wrong on both sides and by shame on ours—theirs was not capable of shame. They had many friends and only one formidable enemy—themselves.

The Americans met them with the sword in one hand and the olive branch in the other. They declined the branch and defied the sword. The English offered them gifts in both hands, and they took all that was offered, rendering in exchange services disgraceful to the more civilized party to the contract. The French offered them love, and won theirs in return. While other whites held aloof, the gay Frenchman fraternized with them, became one with them, shared their lives and their pursuits, won their religious allegiance—nay, more; in a gentler and more irresistible way prevailed over them, for he formed with their women alliances which furnished the inferior race a hybrid, partly like themselves, but superior, and able and willing to be their leaders against the more grasping, less loving Americans. These hybrids have, in many cases, continued the race on its enlightened side, and there are not wanting among ourselves splendid specimens of manhood and womanhood, whose fine figures, flashing eyes, and strong, grave faces, proclaim the proud possession of the blood of the only really "first citizens" of our democratic republic.

It is now hard to trace the Indians who departed hence in 1835, fifty-eight years ago. They are almost "lost tribes." The report for 1890 of the Commissioners of Indian Affairs, gives Pottowatomies of various descriptions scattered in many places. This same is true of the Ottawas and Chippewas.

The larger part of the Pottowatomies (known of old as the "Woods Band," in contradistinction to the "Prairie Band") have renounced tribal relations and are known as the "Citizen Band." They number scarcely two thousand souls, and occupy a tract nearly thirty miles square (575,000 acres) in Oklahoma.

The Commissioners' report says but little about them, giving more attention to the "Prairie Band," since they are still a tribe, and thus, "wards of the nation." They number only 432, and hold in common 77,357 acres in Kansas, where they are doing fairly, but are pestered with the dregs of the "Citizen Band," who fall back on the tribe like the returned prodigal—but unrepentant, and still fit company only for the husk-eating swine.

Of the "Citizen Band," Special Agent Porter says:

"The Pottowatomies are citizens of the United States, thoroughly tinctured with white blood. Nearly all of them speak English and read and write. Some of them are quite wealthy, being good farmers, with large herds of stock. Their morals are below the standard, considering their advanced state as a civilized' people."

This is not high praise; still, it gives hope for better things. Peace and industry coming first, civilization and morality will follow. The savage Indian is essentially a being of the past (notwithstanding the survival of a few wild Apaches, a few "ghost-dancers" among the Sioux, and some other exceptional bodies) and he is succeeded by the truly civilized Indian (of whom the Cherokees are a splendid example), a self-respecting, self governing, self-educating, prosperous human being; not particularly different from the frontiers-man, except by a slight and diminishing shade of color and by the possession of the best characteristics of his savage ancestors. It may perhaps be said that no race of men has ever made as much progress in five generations as have the "civilized Indians." It is only one hundred and sixty years since d'Artaguiette, Vinsenne, the Jesuit Senat, and young St. Ange, son of the French commandant in the Illinois country (Fort Chartres), were defeated in the Arkansas country and were burned at the stake by the unconquered Chickasaws, who were "amazed to see the fortitude with which white men could die." And now, in the territory adjoining Arkansas on the west, the descendants of the torturers are cultivating farms, maintaining governments, courts, schools and churches, and in short, setting an example worthy to be followed by many who have been "civilized" from the time ages back of the year 1492; when the innocent, luckless Haytians learned of the existence of the unspeakable Spaniards, in cruelty the only rivals of the North American aborigines.

What is the reason for the intense interest and curiosity which clusters about this story of violence and rapine, of heroism, anguish and death? Other massacres have blotted with blood the pages of American history. From Deerfield and Schenectady to the Little Bighorn, our devoted bands have perished at the hands of the American Indian; and each dark day is suffered to rest as a mere tradition, buried in the half-forgotten folk-lore of its time and place. Why does the Fort Dearborn massacre, involving only a few score souls, hold a different rank in our hearts?

It is because the footsteps of millions are passing over the spot where it all happened; steamers are churning its peaceful waters; bells and steam-whistles are rending the air that bore away the sound of gun-shots, war-whoops and dying cries; and the sculptors' art is putting into immortal bronze the memory of its incidents. Thus does it gain an *ex post facto* importance and a posthumous fame.

Contemporaneous Reports 107

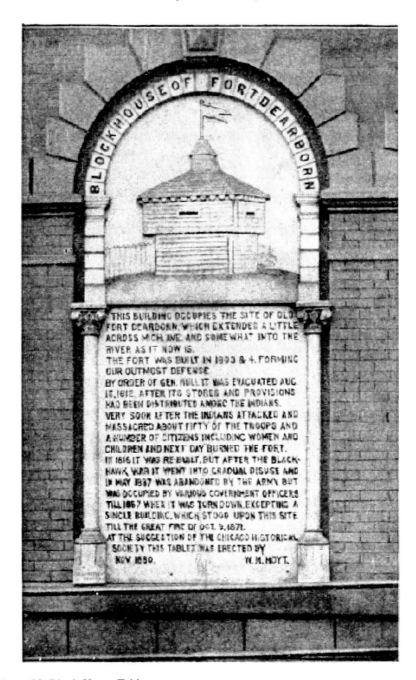

Figure 23. Block-House Tablet.

Figure 24. Beaubien Fiddle and Calumet, In Possession of the Calumet Club.

Among the world's great cities, Chicago should be the one most thoroughly recorded. No other that counts her denizens by the million has among them those born before her annals fairly began. No other has had such startling vicissitudes. Laid low by slaughter in her infancy and by fire in her youth, she has climbed with bounding steps, upward and onward. Toiling, enduring, laughing, prospering, exulting; she has taken each scourge as a fillip to her energy, each spur as a stimulus to her courage. Hers is the enthusiasm of youth with the strength of maturity.

The early days of Paris and London are lost in half-mythical shadow. Even if told, their incidents might fail to match in interest those which have befallen their young sister. So much the more zealously should we who love this youthful aspirant for fame, take care that the romance of her childhood shall be preserved and handed down to posterity.

The spirited figure of La Salle (given by Lambert Tree) and Martin Ryerson's Indian group, are both fine memorials of the dawn of things in the North-West. Eli Bates's matchless statue of Lincoln is devoted to a page in the history of the whole Union. Now comes Chicago's latest treasure, the magnificent group commemorating the massacre of 1812; a purely civic work, to keep in the minds of Chicago's citizens, for untold generations, the romance and reality of her struggling infancy.

Honor to the men who, in the intense pressure of the present, still have thoughts for the past and the future.

At the unveiling, (1881) of the Block-House Tablet (designed by the Chicago Historical Society) set by William M. Hoyt in the north wall of his warehouse, facing Rush Street Bridge from the south, Mr. Eugene Hall read some stanzas of original verse so musical, so poetic and so apt for the occasion, that I venture (with his permission) to repeat them here, as a finish to our story.

FORT DEARBORN, CHICAGO, 1881

Here, where the savage war-whoop once resounded, Where council fires burned brightly years ago, Where the red Indian from his covert bounded To scalp his pale-faced foe:

Here, where grey badgers had their haunts and burrows, Where wild wolves howled and prowled in midnight bands, Where frontier farmers turned the virgin furrows, Our splendid city stands.

Here, where brave men and helpless women perished, Here, where in unknown graves their forms decay; This marble, that their memory may be cherished, We consecrate today.

No more the farm-boy's call, or lowing cattle. Frighten the timid wild fowl from the slough: The noisy trucks and wagons roll and rattle O'er miles of pavement now.

Now are our senses startled and confounded. By screaming whistle and by clanging bell. Where Beaubien's merry fiddle once resounded When summer twilight fell.

Here stood the fort with palisades about it. With low log block-house in those early hours; The prairie fair extended far without it. Blooming with fragrant flowers.

About this spot the buildings quickly clustered; The logs decayed, the palisade went down. Here the resistless Western spirit mustered And built this wondrous town.

Here from the trackless plain its structures started. And one by one, in splendor rose to view. The white ships went and came, the years departed, And still she grandly grew.

Till one wild night, a night each man remembers. When round her homes the red fire leaped and curled. The sky was filled with flame and flying embers. That swept them from the world.

Men said: "Chicago's bright career is ended!" As by the smouldering stones they chanced to go, While the wide world its love and pity blended, To help us in our woe.

O where was ever human goodness greater? Man's love for man was never more sublime. On the eternal scroll of our Creator 'Tis written for all time.

Chicago lives, and many a lofty steeple Looks down today upon this western plain; The tireless hands of her unconquered people Have reared her walls again.

Long may she live and grow in wealth and beauty, And may her children be, in coming years, True to their trust and faithful in their duty As her brave pioneers.

APPENDIX A.

JEAN BAPTISTE POINTE DE SAIBLE, THE HAYTIAN NEGRO WHO WAS THE FIRST "WHITE MAN" TO SETTLE IN CHICAGO (1776-77)

Figure 25. Cock-Crow.

Not in jest, but in grave, sober earnest, the Indians used to say that "the first white man in Chicago was a n*gger." In their view, all non-Indians were "whites," the adjective having to them only a racial significance. Then, too the aborigines had no jests—no harmless ones. Peering into the dim past for early items concerning what is now Chicago, one comes first to the comparatively clear (though positively scanty) records of the French—La Salle, Marquette, Tonti, Hennepin, St. Cosme and their bold associates—who came in by way of the St. Lawrence in the seventeenth century—1672 to 1700.

From that time there occurs a great blank. Scarcely a ray of light or word of intelligence pierces the deep gloom for just one hundred years. Detroit, Mackinaw, Lake Superior, Green Bay, Fort Duquesne and St. Louis are kept in view. Even Kaskasia and Fort Chartres, both in Illinois territory, are on record; a circumstance due to the fact, not generally known, that they were points of importance in John Law's famous Mississippi scheme. But Chicago was almost as though it had sunk below the waves of Lake Michigan when La Salle, Marquette and St. Cosme bade it good-bye.

Figure 26. Robert Cavelier, Sieur De La Salle.

Appendix A. 115

Suddenly, in 1778, in the midst of the Revolutionary War, the name reappears in literature in a curious way. It comes to us through a poetical allusion from the pen of Colonel Arent Schuyler de Peyster, commandant at Michilimackinac. De Peyster, as his name suggests, was a New Yorker of the ancient Dutch stock He entered the English army and in 1757 was commissioned lieutenant in the Eighth, or King's Regiment of Foot. Necessarily he was and continued to be a royalist, and when war broke out served King George against Gen. George.

Figure 27. George Rogers Clark (Late in Life). From "Cyclopædia of United States History."—Copyright 1881, by Harper & Brothers.

Fortunately for our knowledge of the West during Revolutionary times, Colonel de Peyster was a scholar and a gentleman as well a soldier and a Tory He left a volume of "Miscellanies," which was first published (1813) in Dumfries, Scotland, whither the old soldier retired when the bad cause for which he made a good fight came to a disastrous end by the peace of Paris in 1783.[36] An edition, edited by General J. Watts de Peyster, of Yonkers, was published in 1888.

---

[36] After his return to Scotland, Colonel de Peyster commanded the "fencibles" (militia), of which Robert Burns was a member, and it was in his honor that the poet wrote his poem, "To Colonel de Peyster," beginning:
"My honored Colonel, deep I feel Your interest in the poets' weal."
and ending, after several stanzas:

Colonel de Peyster's post of loyal service was Mackinaw, whither, as the "Miscellanies" tell us, he was sent early in 1774, "to command the post, with the painful task of superintending the lake Indians." "Canoes arrived with passes signed by the American General Wooster, and Dr. Benjamin Franklin, wherein it was stipulated that those traders should not afford any succor whatever to the British garrison."

He adds that "in the spring following they [the Indians] were sent down to assist General Burgoine in his expedition across Lake Champlaine"—an entry which recalls the fate of poor Jane McCrea, whose death at the hands of the Indians, near Saratoga, used to draw tears from our childish eyes in the good old times before patriotism was no more.

In that expedition they seem to have done no valuable service to King George (except the killing of Miss McCrea), and on their return they were assembled at Mackinaw for the purpose of making a diversion in favor of the English General Hamilton, whom George Rogers Clark, our paragon of Western soldiers, had defeated already (though de Peyster did not know it) and sent across the Alleghanies, a prisoner, to Patrick Henry, Governor of Virginia.

Now comes in the mention of Chicago. De Peyster made a speech to the assembled redskins, which speech he next day turned into rude rhyme at the request of a fair lady whom he calls, in gallant French phrase, "une chère compagne de voyage." The poem is included in the "Miscellanies."[37]

The entire versified speech is too long to quote, interesting though it be as an unstudied sketch of things of that time and place. Any one wishing to know more of it can find it in the "Miscellanies," of which a copy should be easily found in any large library.

"But lest you think I am uncivil To plague you with this draunting drivel. Abjuring a intentions evil, I quat my pen:
The Lord preserve us frae the devil, Amen! Amen!"

[37] The lady was his wife. The marriage was childless, and General J. Watts de Peyster (1892) says in a private note: "She was *chère* indeed to de P's lineal heirs, for her cajolery of the Colonel transferred his property from his nephew, protege and namesake. Captain Arent Schuyler de Peyster, to her own people, McMurdo's, or whatever was the name of her nephews." General de Peyster says that he himself got the story from Captain Arent Schuyler de Peyster, the namesake in question, and the discoverer of the "De Peyster Islands," in the Pacific Ocean.

Appendix A. 117

SPEECH TO THE WESTERN INDIANS

Great chiefs, convened at my desire To kindle up this council-fire, Which, with ascending smoke shall burn, Till you from war once more return To lay the axe in earth so deep That nothing shall disturb its sleep.

I know you have been told by Clark His riflemen ne'er miss the mark; In vain you hide behind a tree If they your finger-tip can see. The instant they have got their aim Enrolls you on the list of lame.

But then, my sons, this boaster's rifles, To those I have in store are trifles: If you but make the tree your mark The ball will twirl beneath the bark. Till it one-half the circle find, Then out and kill the man behind.

Clark says, with Louis in alliance He sets your father at defiance; That he, too, hopes, ere long, to gain Assistance from the King of Spain.

Suppose, awhile, his threats prove true. My children, what becomes of you? Your sons, your daughters and your wives, Must they be hacked by their big knives? Clark, soon repulsed, will ne'er return, While your war-fire thus clear doth burn.

At Fort St. Joseph and the Post, Go, lay in ambush for his host, While I send round Lake Michigan And raise the warriors to a man. Who, on their way to get to you. Shall take a peep at Eschikagou.[38]

Those runagates at Milwackie Must now perforce with you agree. Sly Siggernaak and Naakewoin Must with Langlade their forces join, Or he will send them, *tout au diable* As he did Baptiste Pointe de Saible.[39]

So steps upon the stage of history the earliest non-Indian settler of Chicago; a man who built, at about the time of our Declaration of Independence, the house which was standing within the memory of hundreds of Chicagoans of 1892—the well-known "Kinzie Mansion," that faced the north bank of the river where Pine Street now ends.

Mrs. John H. Kinzie, in her delightful book, "Wau-Bun, the Early day in the North-West," calls him "Pointe au Sable," and says he was a native of San Domingo, and came from that island with a friend named

---

[38] A river and fort at the head of Lake Michigan.
[39] A handsome negro, well educated and settled in Chicago, but much in the interest of the French.

Glamorgan; who had obtained large Spanish grants in or about St. Louis. She adds that Jean Baptiste sold his Chicago establishment to a French trader named Le Mai, and went back to Peoria where his friend Glamorgan was living, and died tinder his roof, presumably about 1800. From Le Mai, the property passed in 1803, to John Kinzie, the real pioneer of Chicago.

Hispaniola (Hayti and San Domingo) was discovered and even colonized, by Columbus, in 1492. It had then some two million inhabitants, living like our first parents in Eden (Genesis I, 27), but the unspeakable cruelty of the Spaniards so depopulated the splendid and happy island, that in 1517—twenty-five years later—it was requisite to import negro slaves to carry on the mining, and to-day not one soul of the original race survives.

The French began to come in 1630, and by the treaty of Ryswick [1697] the island was divided between France and Spain. Then began the greatness of the Haytian negro, which culminated in Toussaint L'Ouverture, liberator of his race from French slavery and his land from French domain; and later, victim to Napoleon's perfidy. Under the French rule many free negroes were educated in France, very probably Baptiste Pointe de Saible among the rest. At any rate he was of the adventurous spirit which would rather be first in a new sphere than last in an old, and so, with Glamorgan, he came over to Mobile or New Orleans. Then (probably on one of John Law's "Compagnie de l'Occident" bateaux) he came up the Mississippi to Kaskaskia, Cahokia, St. Louis, and at last to Peoria, on the Illinois, where he left Glamorgan, and pushed on to the Pottowatomie outposts where we find him in 1778, the object of Colonel de Peyster's admiring dislike.

Edward G. Mason, in an address before the Historical society, gives a tradition in regard to Pointe de Saible's welcome on Chicago soil, which tradition appears in "Early Western Days," a volume published by John T. Kingston, formerly a state senator of Wisconsin. It runs thus: An Indian living south of the Portage River—now called the Chicago—being out hunting, suddenly came upon a strange object, half hidden by the underbrush. It was a black face with white eyes and woolly hair! (Probably no Indian of his tribe had ever seen a negro.) After gazing at the novel sight awhile, he grunted, "Ugh! Mucketewees!" (black meat.) He captured the odd animal and carried him to the village, whither came the Indians from far and near to gaze, to wonder, and to speculate. Fortunately for Baptiste, for Chicago and for history, the consensus of opinion called it "bad meat," and so the creature's life was spared.

Shaubena, a chief of the Pottowatomies, was in and about Chicago long after their war dance of 1836. He had seen Pointe de Saible, but unfortunately his knowledge concerning him is not on record. Mr. Mason says regretfully:

> In 1855, at the old Wells Street station, I saw old Shaubena wearing moccasins, leggins, coat and plug hat with colored strings tied around it. He was gazing with great delight at the Galena Railway engine, named for him, and calling the attention of the people on the platform to it. He doubtless thought that a much more wonderful sight than old Jean Baptiste.

Figure 28. Shaubena in Old Age. (About 1856.)

One other mention of Pointe de Saible is thrown up from the almost barren shore of Western history. The third volume of the Wisconsin Historical Society's collection contains certain "Recollections" of Augustin Grignon (a grandson of Sieur Charles de Langlade), who became the first permanent white settler of Wisconsin about 1735, and, as we have seen, is named by de Peyster in his verses, among which "Recollections" occurs the following precious bit:

"At a very early period there was a negro who lived here (Chicago) named Baptiste Pointe de Saible. My brother, Perish Grignon, visited Chicago about 1794 and told me that Pointe de Saible was a large man, that he had a commission for some office, but for what particular office or for what government I cannot now recollect. He was a trader, pretty wealthy, and drank freely. I do not know what became of him."

With these bits of chance allusion—touches here and there—we get a quite distinct impression of the lonely Baptiste. His origin shows possibility of greatness, for it was the same with that of François Dominique Toussaint, surnamed l'Ouverture. Like him, he was a French West-Indian mulatto. He was large, handsome, well-educated and adventurous, traits which mark pretty clearly his migrations and his fortunes. Neither in Mobile, New Orleans, Kaskaskia, nor St. Louis could he probably feel at home, for at each of these places nigritude was associated with servitude. Among the Peoria Indians he probably found scanty elbow-room, especially if his friend and rival trader, Glamorgan, was, as his name implies, of Welsh blood—a race which gleans close, and thrives where others starve.

Not unnaturally would he, as tradition suggests, aspire to headship of the great tribe of Pottowatomies, for he knew how vastly superior he was to the best of them; and quite as naturally would he fail, seeing that the red strain of blood and the black have even less in common than has each with the white. At the same time, considering the state of domestic relations at that time and place, we may be very sure that he did not fail to "take some savage woman"—one or more—to rear his dusky race in large numbers and much rude, half-breed gaiety and contentment.

As to his office, one would like greatly to know something about it, and is prone to wish that somebody would look it up—in the general government archives, or those of the North-West Territory, which had been established in 1788, General St. Clair being its first governor, and Cincinnati (Losantiville) its capital. Why should it not have been under Harrison and Wells? It would scarcely have been an English office in view of the unpleasant allusion by de Peyster, though the English maintained emissaries hereabouts—fomenters of discontent—away on almost to the war of 1812. Still, it might be worthwhile to try the Canadian records. Barring swell a discovery, it seems probable that the last word has been written about him.

Jean Baptiste's name "Pointe de Saible" (or Sable) might be suspected of being a description of his residence rather than an inheritance from his forefathers, for the cabin of squared logs, so early built and so lately destroyed, stood at the head of the great sand-point which of old interrupted the course of the Chicago river lakeward, and turned it south for about half a mile to where it flowed over a long, fordable, narrow bar formed by the ceaseless sandstream that moves from north to south along the western shore of Lake Michigan. But the records and traditions are old enough and exact enough to uphold the name as a patronymic, and leave the place as a mere coincidence. One might almost as easily trace it to his lack of grit and perseverance, seeing that he put his hand to the plow and looked back; that he came to Chicago in hope and moved away in despair; that having a "homestead location" he did not stay and "prove up;" that, owning, by occupation, a thousand million dollars worth of real estate, he sold it for a song instead of waiting for a "boom." *Point de sable*—"no sand."

The two other characteristics of Chicago's first merchant-prince, which are preserved for us by lucky chance, are that he was "pretty wealthy" and that he "drank freely." Only one of these traits has come down to his successors of a century later. [From "Liber Scriptorum," published by the Authors' Club, New York.]

Figure 29. Chicago River. Junction of North and South Branches (1830).

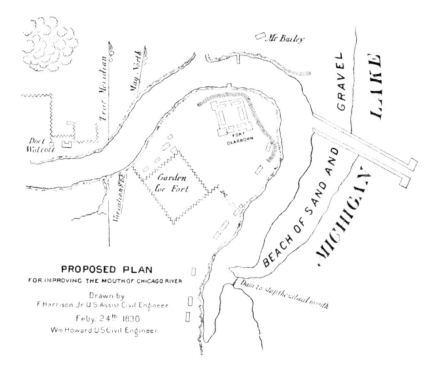

APPENDIX B.

FORT DEARBORN RECORDS AT WASHINGTON

War Department records, back of the war of 1812, are few and poor; partly, no doubt, for the reason that during that short struggle a British force, sailing up the Potomac, seized upon the defenceless little city of

Washington and burned its public buildings with their contents. The Hon. Robert Lincoln, Secretary of War (under President Garfield) at the time of unveiling the Block House Tablet, May 21, 1881, kindly furnished to Mr. Wentworth copies of all documents on file relating to Fort Dearborn and its garrison, (Fergus' Hist., Series No. 16.)

Extract from a letter written June 28, 1804, by General Henry Dearborn, Secretary of War under President Jefferson:

> Being of opinion that, for the general defence of our country, we ought not to rely upon fortifications, but on men and steel; and that works calculated for resisting batteries of cannon are necessary only for our principal seaports, I cannot conceive it useful or expedient to construct expensive works for our interior military posts, especially such as are intended merely to hold the Indians in check. I have therefore directed stockade works aided by block-houses to be erected at Vincennes, at Chikago, at or near the mouth of the Miami of the lakes, and at Kaskaskia, in conformity with the sketch herewith enclosed, each calculated for a full company; the block-houses to be constructed of timber slightly hewed, and of the most durable kind to be obtained at the respective places; the magazines for powder to be of brick, of a conic figure, each capable of receiving from fifty to one hundred barrels of powder. Establishments of the kind here proposed will, I presume, be necessary for each of the military posts in Upper and Lower Louisiana, New Orleans and its immediate dependencies excepted. I will thank you to examine the enclosed sketch, and to give me your opinion on the dimensions and other proposed arrangements You will observe the block-houses are to be so placed as to scour from the upper and lower stories the whole of the lines. The back part of the barracks are to have port-holes which can be opened when necessary for the use of musketry for annoying an enemy.
>
> It will, I presume, be proper ultimately to extend palisades round the block-houses.

Statement compiled from the Records of the Adjutant General's office in the case of Fort Dearborn, with copies of orders:

Appendix B. 125

Fort Dearborn, situated at Chicago, Ill., within a few yards of Lake Michigan. Latitude 41° 51' North; Longitude 87° 15' West. Post established by the United States forces in 1804. (From 1804-12 no records are on file.)

August 15th, 1812, the garrison having evacuated the post and were *en route* for Ft. Wayne, under the command of Captain Nathan Heald, 1st U. S. Infantry, composed of 54 Regular Infantry, 12 Militia men, and one interpreter, was attacked by Indians to the number of between 400 and 500, of whom 15 were killed. Those of the garrison killed were Ensign George Ronan, 1st Infantry, Dr. Isaac Van Voorhis, Captain Wells, Interpreter, 24 enlisted men, U S. Infantry, and 12 Militia-men; 2 women and 12 children were also killed. The wounded were Captain Nathan Heald and Mrs. Heald. None others reported. The next day, August 16th, 1812, the post was destroyed by the Indians. Reoccupied about June 1816, Capt. Hezekiah Bradley, 3rd Infantry, commanding. The troops continued in occupation until October, 1823, when the post was evacuated and left in charge of the Indian agent; It was reoccupied Oct. 3rd, 1828.

Capt. Hezekiah Bradley, 3rd Infantry, commanded the post from June 1816, to May 1817, Brevet Major D. Baker to June 1820; Captain Hezekiah Bradley, 3rd Infantry, to January 1821, Major Alex Cummings, 3rd Infantry, to October, 1821; Lieut. Col. J. McNeal, 3rd Infantry, to July 1823; Captain John Greene, 3rd Infantry, to October, 1823; post not garrisoned from October 1823, to October 1828. No returns of post on file prior to 1828.

COPIES OF ORDERS

Order No. 35

Adjutant General's Office, Washington, 27 May, 1823.

The Major-General commanding the army directs that Fort Dearborn, Chicago, be evacuated, and that the garrison thereof be withdrawn to the headquarters of the 3rd regiment of Infantry.

One company of the 3rd regiment of Infantry will proceed to Mackinac and relieve the company of artillery now stationed there, which, with the company of artillery at Fort Shelby, Detroit, will be withdrawn and ordered to the harbor of New York.

The commanding General of the Eastern department, will give the necessary orders for carrying these movements into effect, as well as for the security of the public property at Forts Dearborn and Shelby.

By order of Major-General Brown.

(Signed) Chas. J. Nourse, *Act'g Adjutant-General.*

Order No. 44

Adjutant-General's Office, Washington, 19 August, 1828.

(Extract.) In conformity with the directions of the Secretary of War, the following movements of the troops will be made.

Two companies of the 5th regiment of Infantry to reoccupy Fort Dearborn, at the head of Lake Michigan; the remaining eight companies to proceed by the way of the Wisconsin and Fox rivers to Fort Howard, Green Bay, where the headquarters of the regiment will be established.

Four Co's of the Reg't to constitute the garrison of Fort Howard; two Co's for the garrison of Michilimackinac, and two for that of Fort Brady.

4. The Quartermaster-General's department to furnish the necessary transportation and supplies for the movement and accommodation of the troops.

The subsistence department to furnish the necessary supplies of provisions.

The Surgeon-General to supply medical officers and suitable hospital supplies for the posts to be established and reoccupied.

5. The Commanding Generals of the Eastern and Western departments are respectively charged with the execution of this order as far as relates to their respective commands.

By order of Major General Macomb, Major-General Commanding the Army.

(Signed) R. Jones, *Adjutant-General.*

Order No. 16

Adjutant-General's Office, Washington, 23 Feb., 1832.

(Copy.) The headquarters of the 2nd Regiment of Infantry are transferred to Fort Niagara. Lieut. Col. Cummings, with all the officers and men composing the garrison of Madison Barracks, Sackett's Harbor, will accordingly relieve the garrison of Fort Niagara; and Major Whistler, on being relieved by Lieut.-Col. Cummings, with all the troops under his command, will repair to Fort Dearborn (Chicago, Illinois) and garrison that post.

Assistant Surgeon De Camp, now on duty at Madison Barracks, is assigned to duly at Fort Dearborn, and will accompany the troops ordered to that post. These movements will take place as soon as the navigation will permit.

By order of Major-General Macomb.

(Signed) R. Jones, *Adjutant-General*.

GENERAL ORDER HEADQUARTERS OF THE ARMY. NO. 80

Adjutant-General's Office, Washington, Nov. 30th, 1836.

(Extract) I. The troops stationed at Fort Dearborn, Chicago, will immediately proceed to Fort Howard and join the garrison at that post. Such public property as may be left at Fort Dearborn will remain in charge of Brevt-Major Plympton, of the 5th Infantry; who will continue in command of the post until otherwise instructed.

By order of Alexander Macomb, Maj.-Gen. Com'd'g-in-Chief.

(Signed) R. Jones, *Adjutant-General*.

Figure 30. Interior of New Fort (1850), Lake House in the Distance.

When the last fort was being demolished [1856] an old paper was found which bore internal evidence of being a survival from the first fort. How it could have survived the flames of 1812 is a mystery. Perhaps some brick bomb-proof magazine chanced to shelter it, and the builders of the new fort, finding it, laid it in a closet, where it remained, hidden and forgotten. One would like to see it to-day—if it also survived October 9, 1871!

> Permission is hereby given for one gill of whiskey each: Denison,[A] Dyer,[A] Andrews,[A] Keamble (?), Burman, J. Corbin,[A] Burnett, Smith,[A] McPherson, Hamilton, Fury[A], Grumond[A] (?), Morfitt, Lynch,[A] Locker,[A] Peterson,[A] P. Corbin,[A] Van Horn,[40] Mills.

(Signed), *G Ronan,*
November 12th, 1811.

---

[40] Appear on the nuster-roll given. Several of the names recur in the Plattsburg story of the nine survivors (21 May 1814).

Appendix B. 129

On December 29, 1836, the garrison was finally withdrawn from Fort Dearborn, and after its thirty-three years of stirring vicissitudes it passed into a useless old age, which lasted a score of years before its abandonment as a government possession. In fact, one of its buildings—a great, barn-like, wooden hospital—was standing, in use as a hospital storehouse, up to 1871, when the great fire obliterated it, with nearly all else that was ancient in Chicago.

Figure 31. Waubansa Stone with Great Fire Relics.

An exception to this destruction and the fast gathering cloud of oblivion, is to be found in an old red granite boulder, with a rude human face carved on it, which stood in the center of the fort esplanade, and which is now (1891) one of our few antiquarian treasures. It is nearly eight feet high by three feet in greatest diameter, and weighs perhaps 4,000 pounds. In prehistoric times the Indians used the concave top for a corn-mill, and for many, many weary hours must the patient and long-suffering squaws have leaned over it, crushing the scanty, flinty corn of those days into material for the food of braves and pappooses.

Many persons have looked on it as a relic of prehistoric art—the sacrificial stone of an Aztec teocalli perhaps—but Mr. Hurlbut gives the cold truth; more modern, though scarcely less romantic. He says it was set up in the fort, and soldiers, sick and well, used it as a lounging-place. Sometimes it served as a pillory for disorderly characters, and it was a common expression or threat, that for certain offenses the offender would be "sent to the rock." Waubansa was a Chicago chief, and a soldier-sculptor tried to depict his features on the stone; and (to quote Mr. Hurlbut):

"The portrait pleased the Indians, the liege friends of the chief, greatly; for a party of them, admitted into the block-house to see it, whooped and leaped as if they had achieved a victory, and with uncouth gestures they danced in a triumphant circle around the rock."

> In 1837 ... Daniel Webster paid a visit to the West, and took Chicago in his route.... The conveyance was a barouche with four elegant creams attached. Mr. Webster was accompanied by his daughter and son. Every wheel-vehicle, every horse and mule in town, it is said, were in requisition that day, and the senator was met some miles out by a numerous delegation from this *new city*, who joined in the procession.... It was the fourth of July, the column came over Randolph Street bridge, and thence to the parade-ground within the fort. There were guns at the fort, which were eloquent, of course, though the soldiers had left some weeks before. The foundation of all this outcry about Mr. Webster is, that the base and platform on which that gentleman stood when he made the speech within the fort, was the rock, the same Waubansa stone.... Justin Butterfield (who stood directly in front of the senator) swung his hat and cheered the speaker.

The "statue" was pierced to form the base of a fountain, and was set up as one of the curiosities of the great Sanitary Commission Fair, held in 1865, in Dearborn Park, in aid of the sick and wounded in the war for the Union. In 1856 it was adopted as a relic by the Hon. Isaac N. Arnold—

member of Congress during the war and one of the staunchest and ablest of patriots, and most devoted of friends to the soldiers—who moved it to his home, in Erie street. Mr. Arnold's house was burned with the rest in the great fire of 1871, and old "Waubansa" passed through the flames with the same unmoved look he had preserved through his earlier vicissitudes. Afterward numerous fire relics were grouped about him and a photograph taken, wherein, for the first time, he looks abashed, as if conscious of the contrast between his uncouthness and the carvings which surround his antique lineaments. The stone stands open to the public view in the grounds adjoining the new home (100 Pine Street), which Mr. Arnold built after the fire, and in which he lived up to the time of his lamented death, in April, 1884.

Who were the victims of August fifteenth, 1812? What were the names of the killed, the wounded, the tortured, the missing? This is a question to which only the merest apology for an answer can be given. In tens of thousands of cases the very act of dying for one's country forbids the possibility of becoming known to fame. Nameless graves dot our land from north to south, and from east to west, especially from the Susquehanna to the Rio Grande and from the Ohio to the Gulf. Heaven knows who were those dead, and who they might have become if they had not died when and where they did. Let us hope that somewhere in the universe they have their record—on earth they are forgotten.

I have aimed at recording every surviving name of the dwellers in Chicago up to the massacre. As an effort toward that end, I give, on the next page, the last muster and pay-roll of the troops at the old fort, as shown by existing records. It is headed:

"Muster roll of a company of Infantry under the command of Captain Nathan Heald, in the First Regiment of the United States, commanded by Colonel Jacob Kingsbury, from Nov. 30, when last mustered, to December 31, 1810."

It concludes with a certificate in the following form, identical, by the way, with the formula in use in our army to this day (1893):

Recapitulation.—Present, fit for duty, 50; sick, 5; unfit for service, 3; on command, 1; on furlough, 1; discharged, 6. Total, 67.

We Certify on honor that this muster-roll exhibits a true statement of the company commanded by Captain Nathan Heald, and that the remarks set opposite their names are accurate and just.

J. Cooper, S. Mate.

Ph. O'Strander, Lieutenant commanding the Company,

Names.	Rank.	Appointed or enlisted.		Remarks and changes since last muster.
*Nathan Heald	Captain	31 Jan.	1807	On furlough in Mass
Philip O'Strander	2nd Lieut.	1 May	1808	{ Present Of Capt. Rhea's Co. Asst M y Agt. Sick.
Seth Thompson	"	18 Aug.	1808	Present
*John Cooper	Surg Mate	13 June	1808	"
Joseph Glass	Sergeant	18 June	1806	"
*John Crozier	"	2 July	1808	"
Richard Rickman	"	10 May	1806	"
Thomas Forth	Corporal	6 July	1807	"
*Asa Campbell	"	26 Jan.	1810	"
*Rhodias Jones	"	9 Dec.	1807	"
* Richard Garner	"	2 Oct.	1810	"
George Burnet	Fifer.	1 Oct.	1806	"
John Smith	"	27 June	1806	"
*John Hamilton	Drummer	5 July	1808	"
*Hugh McPherson	"	20 Oct.	1807	"
*John Allen	Private	27 Nov.	1810	"
George Adams	"	21 Aug.	1806	"
Presley Andrews	"	11 July	1806	" (sick.)
Thomas Ashbrook	"	29 Dec.	1805	Term expired 29 Dec. 1810.
Thomas Burns	"	18 June	1806	Present.
Patrick Burke	"	27 May	1806	" (sick.)

Appendix B. 133

Names.	Rank.	Appointed or enlisted.			Remarks and changes since last muster.
Redmond Berry	"	2	July	1806	"
William Best	"	22	April	1806	Present unfit for service
James Chapman	"	1	Dec.	1805	Time expired 1 Dec. 1810.
James Corbin	"	2	Oct.	1810	Present.
Fielding Corbin	"	7	Dec.	1805	Time expired 7 Dec. 1810.
Silas Clark	"	15	Aug.	1806	On command at Ft. Wayne
James Clark	"	4	Dec.	1805	Time expired 4 Dec. 1810.
*Dyson Dyer	"	1	Oct.	1810	Present (sick).
Stephen Draper	"	19	July	1806	"
*Daniel Dougherty	"	13	Aug.	1807	"
Michael Denison	"	28	April	1806	"
*Nathan Edson	"	6	April	1810	"
*John Fury	"	19	March	1808	"
"Paul Grummo	"	1	Oct.	1810	"
*William N. Hunt	"	18	Oct.	1810	"
John Kelsoe	"	17	Dec.	1808	Time expired 17 Dec. 1810
*David Kennison	"	14	March	1808	Present.
*Sam'l Kirkpatrick	"	20	Dec.	1810	Re-enlisted 20 Dec. 1810.
*Jacob Laudon	"	28	Nov.	1807	Unfit for service.
*James Lutta	"	10	April	1810	....
*Michael Lynch	"	20	Dec.	1810	Re-enlisted 20 Dec. 1810.
*Michael Leonard	"	13	April	1810	Present.
Hugh Logan	"	5	May	1806	"
*Frederick Locker	"	13	April	1810	"
Andrew Loy	"	6	July	1807	"
August Mott	"	9	July	1806	"
Ralph Miller	"	19	Dec.	1805	Term expired 19 Dec. 1810
Peter Miller	"	13	June	1806	Present, unfit for service.
*Duncan McCarty	"	2	Aug.	1807	Present.

Names.	Rank.	Appointed or enlisted.	Remarks and changes since last muster.
Patrick McGowan	"	30 April 1806	"
James Mabury	"	14 April 1806	"
William Moffit	"	23 April 1806	"
John Moyan	"	28 June 1806	"
*John Neads	"	5 July 1808	"
*Joseph Noles	"	8 Sept. 1810	"
*Thomas Poindexter	"	3 Sept. 1810	"
William Pickett	"	6 June 1806	"
*Frederick Peterson	"	1 June 1808	"
*David Sherror	"	1 Oct. 1810	"
*John Suttonfield	"	8 Sept. 1807	"
*John Smith	"	2 April 1808	"
*James Starr	"	18 Nov. 1809	"
Phillip Smith	"	30 April 1806	"
*John Simmons	"	14 March 1810	"
*James Van Home	"	2 May 1810	" (sick).
Anthony L. Waggoner	"	9 Jan. 1806	" (sick).

* Men who are likely to have been in service at the time of the massacre.

Figure 32. Wild Onion.

APPENDIX C.

THE WHISTLER FAMILY

According to Gardner's Military Dictionary, Captain John Whistler was born in Ireland. He was originally a British soldier, and was made prisoner with General Burgoyne at the battle of Saratoga, in 1777, where our General Henry Dearborn was serving as Major. The captives were conducted to Boston, where, by the terms of the capitulation, they should have been paroled; but for some reason (which the English, by considered no sufficient excuse for not complying with the military agreement) the Continental Congress held them as prisoners of war until the peace of 1783.

John Whistler did not return to England, but joined the American army and became first sergeant, and then won his way to a captaincy in the First Infantry, in which capacity he came, in 1804, and built the first Fort Dearborn. He was brevetted major in 1812, and served with his company until it was disbanded after the close of the war (June, 1815). He died in 1827 at Bellefontaine, Missouri, where he had been military storekeeper for several years. John Wentworth (Fort Dearborn; Fergus' Historical Series, No. 16, p. 14) says:

Some writers contend that had Captain Whistler been in charge of the fort instead of Captain Heald, the massacre would not have taken place. Captain Heald has had no one to speak for him here. But he was appointed from Massachusetts a second lieutenant in 1799, and could not be supposed to have that acquaintance with the characteristics of the Indians which Whistler had, who had been in his country's service ever since Burgoyne's surrender in 1777, and principally against the Indians, and frequently participating in the campaigns of General Arthur St. Clair, in one of which he was wounded.

Of him Captain Andreas says (Hist. Chi. Vol. I, p. 80):

After the war he married and settled in Hagerstown, Md., where his son William was born. He enlisted in the American army and took part in the Northwestern Indian War, serving under St. Clair and afterward under Wayne. He was speedily promoted, rising through the lower grades to a lieutenancy in 1792, and became a captain in 1794. He rebuilt the fort in 1815[41] after the destruction and massacre in 1812] and removed to St. Charles, Mo., in 1817. In 1818 he was military storekeeper at St. Louis, and died at Bellefontaine. Mo., in 1827. He was a brave and efficient officer, and became the progenitor of a line of brave and efficient soldiers.

His son, George Washington Whistler, was with Captain John when the family came to Chicago, being then three years old. This is the Major Whistler who became a distinguished engineer in the service of Russia. Another son. Lieutenant William Whistler, with his young wife (Julia Ferson) came to Chicago with Captain Whistler. He will be mentioned later as one of the last commandants of Fort Dearborn, holding that post until 1833. He lived until 1863.

Julia Ferson, who became Mrs. William Whistler, was born in Salem, Mass., 1787. Her parents were John and Mary (La Dake) Ferson. In childhood she removed with her parents to Detroit, where she received most of her education. In May, 1802, she was married to William Whistler

---

[41] Apparently an error. The second fort was built by Captain Hezekiah Bradley, who was sent here for that purpose with two companies of infantry, arriving July 4, 1816.

Appendix C. 137

(born in Hagerstown Md., about 1784), a second lieutenant in the company of his father. Captain John Whistler, U. S. A., then stationed at Detroit. (Fergus' Historical Series No. 16.) She visited Chicago in 1875, when, at eighty-seven, her mind and memory were of the brightest, and conversation with her on old matters was a rare pleasure. Mrs. General Philip Sheridan is her grand niece, and cherishes her relationship as a patent to high rank in our Chicago nobility. No portrait of John Whistler is known to exist. For likenesses of Major and Mrs. William Whistler see pages 58 and 59.

Figure 33. Mrs. Gwenthlean [Whistler] Kinzie (1891).

A daughter of William and this charming old lady was born in 1818, and named Gwenthlean. She was married at Fort Dearborn, in 1834, to Robert A. Kinzie, second son of John Kinzie, the pioneer. Mrs. Gwenthlean Kinzie is now living in Chicago, and has been consulted in the preparation of this narrative.[42]

Mr. Hurlbut (Chicago Antiquities, p. 83) gives the following spirited account of a visit made in 1875 to Mrs. Julia (Ferson) Whistler, wife of William and daughter-in-law of old John, the whilom soldier in the army of General Burgoyne. (It will be observed that Mr. Hurlbut slightly mistook his war record).

> Very few of the four hundred thousand reasonably adult individuals now residing in Chicago are aware that the person of whom we are going to speak is now a visitor in Chicago. After so long a period—since early in the century; before those of our citizens who have reached their "three-score years and ten" were born, when she came, a trustful wife of sixteen, and stepped a shore upon the river-bank—it is not a little remarkable that she is to-day again passing over and around the locality of her early home. Under the gentle supervision of this married maiden's blue eyes our stockade-fortress, then so far within the wilderness, was erected. Yet, of all those who came in that summer of 1803; the sailor-men of that vessel, the oarsmen of that boat, the company of United States soldiers, Captain and Mrs. Whistler and their son, the husband and his bride of a year; all, we may safely say, have bid adieu to earth excepting this lone representative. These are some of the circumstances which contribute to make this lady a personage of unusual interest to the dwellers here. A few particulars in the life of Mrs. Whistler, together with some of the facts attending the coming of those who arrived to assist in the building of Fort Dearborn, will certainly be acceptable.

---

[42] On mentioning to Judge Caton that Mrs Robert Kinzie was again living here following a long absence, the venerable Chief-Justice, after a moment's thought, sad: "Yes, I remember the marriage, and that the bride was one of the most beautiful women you can imagine. I have never seen her since that time. Ladies were not plentiful in this part of the world then, and we were not over particular about looks, but Gwenthlean Whistler Kinzie would be noted for her beauty anywhere at anytime." And on looking at the lady herself, one can well believe all that can be said in praise of her charms in her girlish years—sixteen when she was married.

Appendix C.

It was a coveted pilgrimage which we sought, as any one might believe, for it was during the tremendous rain-storm of the evening of the 29th of October, 1875, that we sallied out to call at Mrs. Colonel R. A. Kinzie's, for an introduction to the lady's mother, Mrs. Whistler. When we entered the parlor, the venerable woman was engaged at the center table, in some game of amusement with her grand-children and great grand-children, seemingly as much interested as any of the juveniles. (We will remark here that five generations in succession of this family have lived in Chicago.) She claimed to enjoy good health, and was, apparently, an unusual specimen of well-preserved faculties, both intellectual and physical. She is of tall form, and her appearance still indicates the truth of the common report, that in her earlier years she was a person of uncommon elegance. A marked trait of hers has been a spirit of unyielding energy and determination, and which length of years has not yet subdued. Her tenacious memory ministers to a voluble tongue, and we may say, briefly, she is an agreeable, intelligent, and sprightly lady, numbering only a little over 88 years. "To-day," said she, "I received my first pension on account of my husband's services." Mrs. Whistler resides in Newport, Kentucky. She has one son and several grandsons in the army. Born in Salem, Mass., July 3rd, 1787, her maiden name was Julia Ferson, and her parents were John and Mary (LaDake) Ferson. In childhood she removed with her parents to Detroit, where she received most of her education. In the month of May, 1802, she was married to William Whistler (born in Hagerstown, Md., about 1784), a second lieutenant in the company of his father, Captain John Whistler, U. S. A., then stationed at Detroit. In the summer of the ensuing year, Captain Whistler's company was ordered to Chicago, to occupy the post and build the fort. Lieutenant James S. Swearingen (late Col. Swearingen of Chillicothe, O.) conducted the company from Detroit overland. The U. S. Steamer "Tracy," Dorr master, was despatched at same time for same destination, with supplies, and having also on board Captain John Whistler, Mrs. Whistler, their son George W., then three years old [afterwards the distinguished engineer in the employ of the Russian government] Lieutenant William Whistler, and the young wife of the last named gentleman. The schooner stopped briefly on her route at the St. Joseph's river, where the Whistlers left the vessel and took a row-boat to Chicago. The schooner, on arriving at Chicago, anchored half a mile from the shore, discharging her freight by boats. Some two thousand Indians visited the locality while the vessel was here, being attracted by so unusual an occurrence as the appearance, in these waters, of a "big canoe with wings." Lieutenant Swearingen returned with the "Tracy" to Detroit.

There were then here, says Mrs. W., but four rude huts or traders' cabins, occupied by white men, Canadian French with Indian wives; of these were Le Mai, Pettell and Ouilmette. No fort existed here at that time, although it is understood (see treaty of Greenville) that there had been one at a former day, built by the French, doubtless, as it was upon one of the main routes from New France to Louisiana, of which extensive region that government long held possession by a series of military posts. [It is said that Durantaye, a French official, built some sort of a fortification here as early as 1685.]

Captain Whistler, upon his arrival, at once set about erecting a stockade and shelter for their protection, followed by getting out the sticks for the heavier work. It is worth mentioning here that there was not at that time within hundreds of miles a team of horses or oxen, and, as a consequence, the soldiers had to don the harness, and with the aid of ropes drag home the needed timbers. The birth of two children within the fort we have referred to elsewhere. Lieutenant Whistler, after a five years' sojourn here, was transferred to Fort Wayne, having previously been made a first lieutenant. He distinguished himself at the battle of Maguago, Mich., August 9th, 1812; was in Detroit at the time of Hull's surrender, and, with Mrs. Whistler, was taken prisoner to Montreal; was promoted to a Captain in December, 1812, to Major in 1826, and to Lieutenant-Colonel in 1845. At his death he had rendered sixty-two years continuous service in the army, yet Mrs. W. says she remembers but six short furloughs during the whole time. He was stationed at various posts, besides those of Green Bay, Niagara, and Sackett's Harbor; at the last named post General Grant (then a subaltern officer) belonged to the command of Colonel W. In June, 1832, Colonel Whistler arrived again at Fort Dearborn, not the work which he had assisted to build twenty-eight years before, for that was burned in 1812, but the later one, erected in 1816-17. He then remained here but a brief period.

Colonel William Whistler's height at maturity was six feet two inches, and his weight at one time was 250 pounds. He died in Newport, Kentucky, December 4th, 1863.

Appendix C.

Captain John Whistler, the builder and commandant of the first Fort Dearborn (afterwards Major W.) was an officer in the army of the Revolution. We regret that we have so few facts concerning his history; nor have we a portrait or signature of the patriot. It is believed that when ordered to Chicago he belonged to a regiment of artillery. He continued in command at Fort Dearborn until the fore part of 1811, we think, for we notice that his successor. Captain Heald, gave to the Pottowatomie chief "Little Chief" a pass to St. Louis, dated July 11, 1811. Mrs. Whistler expressed to us her opinion that had Captain W. been continued in command, the Chicago massacre would not have happened. Major John Whistler died at Bellefontaine. Mo., in 1827.

Colonel James Swearingen was a second lieutenant in 1803, when he conducted the company of Captain Whistler from Detroit across Michigan to Chicago. The regiment of artillery, with which he was connected, is understood to have been the only corps of that branch of defence. Lieutenant Swearingen continued in the service until about 1816, attaining the rank of colonel, when he resigned his commission and made his residence in Chillicothe, O., where he died on his eighty-second birthday, in February, 1864.

Mrs. Julia (Ferson) Whistler died at Newport, Ky., in 1878, at the ripe age of ninety years.

James McNeil Whistler, the eccentric and distinguished London artist, is descended from old John, the Burgoyne British soldier, through George Washington Whistler, the great American engineer in the Russian service.

It is interesting to observe that both our old leading families, the Whistlers and the Kinzies, have furnished successive generations of soldiers to their country. The heroic death of John Harris Kinzie, second, will be noted in the Appendix D, which is devoted to the Kinzie family. Of the Whistlers, some of the name have been constantly in the military service, and when the two families joined by the marriage of Robert Kinzie and Gwenthlean Whistler the racial tendency continued.

General Garland Whistler, son of Colonel William Whistler, was a graduate of West Point, and a soldier in the war for the Union. He is now on the retired list. His son. Major Garland Whistler, also a graduate, was in the late war and is still in the service. Major David Hunter Kinzie, son of

Robert (uniting the two families), left West Point for active service in the Union war. He is now at the Presidio, California. Captain John Kinzie, another son of Robert, is stationed at Omaha.

APPENDIX D.

THE KINZIE FAMILY

Beginning at a point even further back in the dim past than the building of Pointe de Saible's cabin, we take up the narrative of the lives of its latest owners, John Kinzie was born in Quebec about 1763, son of John

McKenzie, or McKinzie, a Scotchman, who married Mrs. Haliburton, a widow, with one daughter,[43] and died when his son John was very young. Mrs. McKenzie made a third marriage, with one William Forsyth, who had served under General Wolfe in the taking of Quebec. William Forsyth, with wife, children and step-children, lived many years in New York, and later in Detroit. While they lived in New York, John McKinzie, afterward John Kinzie, was sent, with two Forsyth half-brothers, to school in Williamsburgh, just across the East river; a negro servant, or slave, going every Saturday night to bring the three boys home. One Saturday there was no Johnnie to be found—the embryo frontiers-man had runaway. He got on board a sloop bound for Albany and fell in with someone who helped him on to Quebec, where he found employment in the shop of a silver-smith; and there he remained three years and learned the trade which later gave him the Indian name, "Shaw-nee-aw-kee"—silver-smith.

We next find him in Detroit, with his mother and step-father, who had moved thither with their Forsyth children.[44] Robert Forsyth, a grandson of William, was well known in Chicago in the decade before the Union War. He was an officer of the Illinois Central Railway, and his tall, handsome figure, his bluff, hearty manners and his unquestionable ability', made him a general favorite.

While at Detroit, John Kinzie began his long career as Indian-trader, beginning with the Shawnees and Ottawas in the Ohio country. In this way

---

[43] This daughter, half-sister of John Kinzie, is said in Wau-Bun to have possessed beauty and accomplishments, and to have lived to become the mother of General Fleming and Nicholas Low, both very well known in New York and Brooklyn.

[44] William Forsyth kept a hotel in Detroit for many years and died there in 1790 Robert, one of his sons, was in the service of the American government during the war of 1812. Thomas, who became Major Thomas Forsyth, U. S. A., was born in Detroit, December 5, 1771. Before the war of 1812, he was Indian Agent among the Pottowatomies at Peoria Lake. After the war of 1812 he was sent as U. S. Indian Agent among the Sauks and Foxes, with whom he remained many years. He died at St. Louis, October 29, 1833. Colonel Robert Forsyth, an early resident of Chicago, was the son of Major Thomas Forsyth; George, another son of William Forsyth, was lost in the woods near Detroit, August 6, 1778. (Andreas' Hist. Chic.) Mrs. Kinzie quotes from the record in an old family Bible, as follows: "George Forsyth was lost in the woods 6th August, 1778, when Henry Hays and Mark Stirling ran away and left him. The remains of George Forsyth we're found by an Indian the 2d of October, 1776 close by the Prairie Ronde." Family tradition gives some particulars of the disaster, adding the touching fact that after its fourteen months' exposure there was nothing to identify the body but the auburn curls and the little boots.

Appendix D.

he made the acquaintance of two Indian girls, who, when young, had been captured on the Kanawha River and taken to Chillicothe, the headquarters of the tribe. Their names were Margaret and Elizabeth McKenzie, and their story is thus romantically told by Rufus Blanchard in his admirable "Discovery of the Northwest and History of Chicago." (R. Blanchard & Co., Wheaton, Ill. 1881.)

> Among the venturesome pioneers of Virginia was a backwoods-man named McKenzie. He, with a number of his comrades, settled at the mouth of Wolf's creek, where it empties into the Kanawha. During Dunmore's War on the frontier [about 1773] the Shawanese, in one of their border forays, came suddenly upon the home of McKenzie, killed his wife and led two of his children into captivity. The names of the young captives were Margaret, ten years old, and Elizabeth; eight years old. They were taken to Chillicothe, the great Indian Town of the Shawanese, where they were adopted into the family of a high-bred Indian chief and raised under the tender care of his obedient squaw, according to custom. Ten years later Margaret was allowed to accompany her foster-father on a hunting-excursion to the St. Mary's River, near Fort Wayne. A young chief of the same tribe became enamored by the graces and accomplishments of the young captive, but Margaret recoiled from her swarthy lover and determined not to yield her heart to one who had no higher destiny for her than to ornament his leggings with porcupine quills—one of the highest accomplishments of which a squaw is capable. Margaret's lover approached the camp where she was sleeping, intending to force her to become his wife. According to the Indian custom, a din of yells and rattle of a drum announced the intentions of the would-be bridegroom to the terrified victim. The heroine fled to the forest for protection.

Figure 34. John K. Clark.

Fortunately her dog followed her as she fled down the bank of the St. Mary's River, to the stockade, half a mile distant, where the horses were kept. The footsteps of her detestable lover were close behind. She turned and set her dog at him, and reached the stockade, unhitched a horse, leaped upon his back and took her flight through the wilderness, seventy-five miles, to her Indian home at Chillicothe. The horse died the next day after he had performed so wonderful a feat without rest or sustenance. This heroic girl and her sister, Elizabeth, became afterward mothers of some of the first pioneers of Chicago.

After the adventures of Margaret, as just told, she, with her sister, Elizabeth, were taken to Detroit by their foster-father, and there they became acquainted with John Kinzie—and they were married. Elizabeth at the same time met a Scotchman named Clark and married him. The

Appendix D. 147

two young couples lived in Detroit about five years, during which time Margaret (Kinzie) had three children, William, James and Elizabeth; and Elizabeth (Clark) had two, John K. and Elizabeth.

Figure 35. Archibald Clybourn.

The treaty of Greenville, 1795, having restored peace on the border, Mr. Isaac McKenzie, the father, received tidings of his children, and went to Detroit to see them. The two young mothers, with their children, returned with their father to their old home, to which arrangement both of their husbands consented. A final separation was not intended, but time and distance divorced them forever. Mr. Kinzie afterwards moved to St. Joseph's, where he married a Mrs. McKillip, the widow of a British officer. Margaret married Mr. Benjamin Hall, of Virginia, and Elizabeth married Mr. Jonas Clybourn of the same place. David, the oldest son of Benjamin Hall and Margaret, made a journey to Chicago in 1822, and he remained there three years. On his return to Virginia his flattering account of the place induced a number of persons to emigrate thither. The first of these was Archibald Clybourn, the eldest son of Elizabeth, who remained a permanent resident and an esteemed citizen, well known to thousands of the present inhabitants of Chicago. His mother was Elizabeth the captive, who, with her second husband, Mr. Clybourn, soon afterwards came to Chicago. Mr. Benjamin Hall was another of the Chicago pioneers who emigrated to Chicago in consequence of David Hall's commendations of its future promise. Margaret, the captive, was his aunt, and to him the writer is indebted for the detail of Margaret's and Elizabeth's history. Mr. Hall is now a resident of Wheaton. He came to Chicago in 1830 and was the proprietor of the first tannery ever established there.

James Kinzie.

Elizabeth Kinzie, daughter of John Kinzie, became the wife of Samuel Miller, of a respectable Quaker family in Ohio. She was highly respected by all who knew her. Her husband kept the Miller House, at the forks of the Chicago River. James Kinzie came to Chicago about 1824, and was well received by his father. [James is mentioned by Mr. Kinzie in a letter written in 1821, given later in this article].

This is the romantic story taken by Mr. Blanchard from the lips of the nephew of one of the captive girls, and given in his valuable history. Some of the circumstances stated as fact may be questionable, especially the "marriage" of the girls to Mr. Kinzie and Mr. Clark. Their summary removal by their father, and their marriage to other men, considered with the marriage of Mr. Kinzie and Mr. Clark to other women, seems to cast doubt upon the occurrence of any ceremonies, civil or religious. Those relations were lightly held at that time and place. There is doubtless a "bend sinister" somewhere, but it seems unlikely that James Kinzie and Elizabeth and Samuel Miller would have left the legitimacy of the more distinguished branch of the family unassailed if it had been assailable. (It is said that Mrs. Miller did chafe under the scandal.)

Appendix D.

Samuel Miller (signature)

In 1800 John Kinzie married Eleanor (Lytle) McKillip, widow of a British officer, who had one daughter, Margaret, afterward Mrs. Lieutenant Helm. In the same year he moved to the St. Joseph's River, which empties into Lake Michigan on its eastern side, nearly opposite Chicago, and there set up his trading-house. His son, John Harris Kinzie, was born at Sandwich, opposite Detroit, where his mother chanced to be spending a day when he made his unexpected appearance.

In 1803 John Kinzie visited Chicago, having probably learned of the approaching establishment of Fort Dearborn, and bought the Le Mai house, built by Jean Baptiste Pointe de Saible, some twenty-five years before. He moved into it with his family in the following year. From that time to his death, in 1828, he is the most conspicuous and unique figure in Chicago history, and fairly deserves the name of the father of the city. His branch trading-posts existed in Milwaukee, at Rock River, on the Illinois and Kankakee Rivers, and in the Sangamon country. To quote again Andreas (Hist. Chic. Vol. I, P. 73):

> This extended Indian trade made the employment of a large number of men at headquarters a necessity, and the Canadian voyageurs in the service of Mr. Kinzie were about the only white men who had occasion to visit Chicago during those early years. He was sutler for the garrison at the fort in addition to his Indian trade, and also kept up his manufacture of the ornaments in which the Indians delighted. During the first residence of Mr. and Mrs. John Kinzie in Chicago, three children were born to them—Ellen Marion in December, 1805; Maria Indiana in 1807, and Robert Allen, February 8, 1810. Margaret McKillip, Mr. Kinzie's step-daughter, who married Lieutenant Linai T. Helm of Fort Dearborn, and also Robert Forsyth, nephew of Mr. Kinzie, were at times members of his family, the latter being the first teacher of John H. Kinzie.

Henry H. Hurlbut in his delightful "Chicago Antiquities,"[45] says:

> By what we learn from a search in the county records at Detroit, John Kinzie seems to have been doing business there in the years 1795-97 and '98. In May, 1795, some portion of the Ottawa tribe of Indians conveyed lands on the Maumee to John Kinzie, silver-smith, of Detroit; also in the same year to John Kinzie, merchant, of Detroit. It appears, also, from the same records, that in September, 1810, John Kinzie and John Whistler Jr. were lately copartners in trade at Fort Dearborn, and in the same year John Kinzie and Thomas Forsyth were merchants in Chicago. We are told by Robert A. Kinzie that his father was sutler at Fort Dearborn when he came to Chicago in 1804; possibly Mr. Whistler Jr. was his partner in that enterprise. In October, 1815, John Kinzie and Thomas Forsyth were copartners in trade in the District of Detroit, Territory of Michigan. In March, 1816, appear on the records the names of John Kinzie, silver-smith, and Elenor, his wife, of Detroit. By these items it seems that though Mr. Kinzie took up his residence in Chicago in 1804 [the first entry here upon his books bore date May 12, 1804] and that he left here after the battle of August, 1812, returning in 1816, yet he was still identified with Detroit, certainly until the summer of 1816. We notice that he was a witness at the treaty of Spring Wells, near Detroit, in September, 1815. He was one of the interpreters.

Wau-Bun gives a long and romantic biography of John Kinzie and his progenitors; such a sketch as would naturally (and properly) be made by a daughter-in-law, writing during the lifetime of many of the persons directly interested in the facts related, but omitting things which would shock the sensibilities of those persons, and mar the literary symmetry of the picture set forth in her pages. She does not allude to the Margaret McKenzie episode, never mentions James Kinzie, well-known Chicagoan as he was, and also ignores another matter which the integrity of history requires to be stated, and which the lapse of almost three generations should disarm of

---

[45] A book full of bits of old-time gossip, traditions and skeptical notes on other traditions, controversial criticism on Wau-Bun and other books, and good-humored raillery, aimed at persons and things of the early day. Only five hundred copies were printed, and the book is becoming scarce, but some copies remain for sale in the family of its author, 27 Winthrop Place, Chicago.

the sting which might attach to it at the time of Wau-Bun. This matter is the killing, in self-defense, of John Lalime, by John Kinzie. (See Appendix F.)

Figure 36. Mrs. Juliette Kinzie (1856). Author of "Wau-Bun."

After the massacre and the subsequent events so romantically described in Wau-Bun, Mr. Kinzie returned, probably in the autumn of 1816, to Chicago, where he reoccupied the historic house. To sit on his front porch and watch the building of a new fort in the old spot must have been a mingling of pleasure and pain. All that had passed since the original incoming of twelve years before must have seemed like a dream. The lake to the eastward, the river in front, the prairie beyond and the oak woods behind him were all as of old; but here around him were the children born and reared in the intervening years; here were new soldiers to take the place of the little band sacrificed four years ago. There, scattered over the sand-hills, were the bleaching bones of the martyred dead, and within dwelt an enduring memory of the horrors of their killing.

Figure 37. John Harris Kinzie (1827). From a miniature in possession of the Kinzie family.

And where were the savings of a lifetime of industry, courage and enterprise? Gone beyond recall. He made heroic efforts to redeem something from the wreck, traveling in Indian fashion and in Indian dress from one to another of the places where he had had branch trading-posts, and where debts were due to him. But it takes only a slight knowledge of affairs in a new country to see clearly that after war has disturbed and

Appendix D.

ravaged a district, and four years of absence have wasted the goods and scattered the debtors, every dollar saved would have cost in the saving two dollars' worth of work and sacrifice of strength and time. That his salvage was small and his later days quite devoid of the ease and comfort which his hard-won early success should have guaranteed him, we have the testimony of a letter written by him August 19, 1821, to his son John H., after he had placed the latter with the American (Astor's) Fur Company at Mackinaw:

> Dear Son—I received your letter by the schooner. Nothing gives me more satisfaction than to hear from you and of you. It does give both myself and your mother a pleasure to hear how your conduct is talked of by every one that hopes you every advantage. Let this rather stimulate you to continue the worthy man, for a good name is better than wealth, and we cannot be too circumspect in our line of conduct. Mr. Crooks speaks highly of you and try to continue to be the favorite of such worthy men as Mr. Crooks, Mr. Stewart and other gentlemen of the firm. Your mother and all of the family are well and send their love to you. James[46] is here, and I am pleased that his returns are such as to satisfy the firm.
>
> I have been reduced in wages, owing to the economy of the government. My interpreter's salary is no more and I have but $100 to subsist on. It does work me hard sometimes to provide for your brothers and sisters on this and maintain my family in a decent manner. I will have to take new measures. I hate to change houses, but I have been requested to wait Conant's arrival. We are all mighty busy, as the treaty commences to-morrow and we have hordes of Indians around us already. My best respects to Mr. Crooks and Stewart and all the gentlemen of your house.
>
> Adieu. I am your loving father,
>
> *John Kenzie*

---

[46] John's half-brother, son of the captive girl, Margaret McKenzie.

This is said to be the only letter of John Kinzie's that is known to exist. (A large and invaluable collection of papers were given in 1877 to the Historical Society by John H. Kinzie, and perished with the society building in the great fire of 1871). No portrait of John Kinzie has ever been found.

He assisted in negotiating the treaty of 1821, before mentioned; addressing the Indians to reconcile them to it, and signing it as a sub-agent, which post he filled under his son-in-law, Dr. Alexander Wolcott, Indian agent. In 1825 he was appointed Justice of the Peace, for Peoria county.

Captain Andreas remarks on John Kinzie's standing with the Indians as follows:

> The esteem in which Mr. Kinzie was held by the Indians is shown by the treaty made with the Pottowatomies September 20, 1828, by one provision of which they gave to Eleanor Kinzie and her four children by the late John Kinzie $3,500 in consideration of the attachment of the Indians to her deceased husband, who was long an Indian trader and who lost a large sum in the trade, by the credits given them and also by the destruction of his property. The money is in lieu of a tract of land which the Indians gave the late John Kinzie long since, and upon which he lived.

There is no doubt that the Indians had a warm feeling for the Kinzies. At the same time it seems probable that the treaty in question, like all other treaties, was carefully arranged by the whites and merely submitted to the Indians for ratification. The Indians did not give any money, all payments came from the United States, and were made to such persons (other than Indians) as the commissioners thought best to care for. As to the land given by the Indians to Mr. Kinzie and on which he lived, where was it? The Indians had parted with the Chicago tract, six miles square, nine years before Mr. Kinzie arrived at Fort Dearborn. It is true that in May, 1795, the Ottawas (not the Pottowatomies) conveyed land in Ohio to John Kinzie and Thomas Forsyth; but he certainly never lived on it. He also lived at Parc-aux-vaches, on the St. Joseph's river, from 1800 to 1804. It is possible, though not probable, that the Indians made him a grant there.

Appendix D.

Figure 38. John Harris Kinzie in Later Life.

Everyone who visited the hospitable "Kinzie mansion" was glad to do so again. Let us follow the good example.

The structure, as put up by Pointe de Saible, and passed through the hands of Le Mai to John Kinzie, was a cabin of roughly squared logs. In Kinzie's time it was beautified, enlarged, improved and surrounded by outhouses, trees, fences, grass plats, piazza and garden. "The latch string hung outside the door,"[47] and all were free to pull it and enter. Friend or stranger,

---

[47] This odd expression of welcome came from the old style of door-fastening; a latch within lifted by the hand or by a string which was poked through a gimlet hole, so that it could be pulled from the outside. To lock the door the household simply pulled in the string and kept it inside.

red-man or white could come and go, eat and drink, sleep and wake, listen and talk as well. A tale is told of two travelers who mistook the house for an inn, gave orders, asked questions, praised and blamed, as one does who says to himself, "Shall I not take mine ease in mine inn?" and who were keenly mortified when they came to pay their scot and found that there was none to pay. In front (as the picture shows) were four fine poplars; in the rear, two great cotton-woods. The remains of one of these last named were visible at a very late period. (Who knows just how lately?) In the outbuildings were accommodated dairy, baking-ovens, stables and rooms for "the Frenchmen," the Canadian engages who were then the chief subordinates in fur-trading, and whose descendants are now well-known citizens, their names perpetuating their ancestry—Beaubien, Laframboise, Porthier, Mirandeau, etc.

Figure 39. Robert Allen Kinzie.

Captain Andreas says:

The Kinzie house was no gloomy home. Up to the very time of their forced removal, the children danced to the sound of their father's violin and the long hours of frontier life were made merry with sport and play. Later the primitive court of Justice Kinzie must have been held in the "spare room"—if spare room there was.

Appendix D.

Hurlbut, in his "Chicago Antiquities," says:

> The last distinguished guest from abroad whom the Kinzies entertained at the old house was Governor Cass; in the summer of 1827. This was during the Winnebago Indian excitement. Gurdon Hubbard says: "While at breakfast at Mr. Kinzie's house we heard singing, faint at first but gradually growing louder as the singer approached. Mr. Kinzie recognized the leading voice as that of Bob Forsyth, and left the table for the piazza of the house, where we all followed. About where Wells Street crosses, in plain sight from where we stood, was a light birch bark canoe, manned with thirteen men, rapidly approaching, the men keeping time with the paddles to one of the Canadian boat-songs; it proved to be Governor Cass and his secretary, Robert Forsyth, and they landed and soon joined in."

The visit of Governor Cass was just before the "Winnebago scare" of 1827. He it was that informed the lonely, unarmed and defenceless post of Fort Dearborn of the Winnebago uprising. Gurdon Hubbard at once proposed to ride down the "Hubbard Trail" for help. The others objected for fear they might be attacked before his return; but it was finally decided that he should go, and go he did. At Danville he raised, within about a day, fifty volunteers, armed and mounted, and started for Fort Dearborn. They reached the Vermilion, then at flood and running "bank-full" and very rapidly. The horses on being driven in would turn and come back to shore. Hubbard, provoked at the delay, threw off his coat, crying: "Give me old Charley!" Mounting the horse he boldly dashed into the stream, and the other horses crowded after him. "The water was so swift that Old Charley became unmanageable; but Hubbard dismounted on the upper side, seized the horse by the mane, and, swimming with his left hand, guided the horse in the direction of the opposite shore. We were afraid he would be washed under, or struck by his feet and drowned, but he got over."[48]

---

[48] See "the Winnebago Scare" by Hiram W. Beckwith, of Danville. Fergus' Historical Series No. 10.

Figure 40. Kinzie Mansion as Given in Wau-Bun.

The brave rescuers arrived and stayed, petted and feasted by the Chicagoans of that day, until a runner came in from Green Bay, bringing word that Governor Cass had made peace with the Indians.

According to Mr. Hurlbut, as the old master neared his end the old homestead also went to decay. The very logs must have been in a perishing condition after fifty years of service, and the lake sand, driven by the lake breezes, piled itself up against the north and east sides. Then, too, the standard of comfort had changed. Son-in-law Wolcott had rooms in the brick building of the unoccupied fort. Colonel Beaubien had a frame house close to the fort's south wall (now Michigan Avenue and River Streets), and thither the Kinzies moved. What more natural than that the ancient tree, as it tottered to its fall, should lean over toward the young saplings that had sprung up at its foot? It is the way of the world.

It was in 1827 that Mr. Kinzie, and whatever then formed his household, quitted the historical log house for the last time. In 1829, it was (says Andreas) used for a while by Anson N. Taylor as a store. In March, 1831, Mr. Bailey lived in it and probably made it the post office, its first location in Chicago, as he was the first postmaster. The mail was then brought from Detroit on horseback, about twice a month.

Figure 41. Gurdon Saltonstall Hubbard, in Middle Life.

Captain Andreas says:

> After 1831 and 1832, when Mark Noble occupied it with his family, there is no record of its being inhabited. Its decaying logs were used by the Indians and immigrants for fuel, and the drifting sands of Lake Michigan was fast piled over its remains. No one knows when it finally disappeared, but with the growth of the new town, this relic of the early day of Chicago passed from sight to be numbered among the things that were.

Mrs. Robert Kinzie says now (1893) that she is sure that the house was standing when she was married in the fort, in 1834, and she thinks long afterward She scouts the idea that those solid logs were used by the Indians or immigrants for fuel.

The following account of Mr. Kinzie's death was learned from Mr. Gurdon S. Hubbard: "He remained in full vigor of health in both body and mind, till he had a slight attack of apoplexy, after which his health continued to decline until his death, which took place in a few months, at the residence of his son-in-law. Dr. Wolcott, who then lived in the brick building, formerly used as the officers' quarters in the fort. Here, while on a brief visit to Mrs. Wolcott (Ellen Marion Kinzie), he was suddenly attacked with apoplexy. Mr. Hubbard, then living in Mr. Kinzie's family, was sent for, and on coming into the presence of the dying man he found him in convulsions on the floor, in the parlor, his head supported by his daughter. Mr. Hubbard raised him to a sitting position and thus supported him till he drew his last breath. The funeral service took place in the fort and the last honors due to the old pioneer were paid with impressive respect by the few inhabitants of the place."

Mr. Kinzie's remains were first buried in the fort burying ground on the lake shore south of the old fort (about Michigan Avenue and Washington Street) whence they were later removed to a plot west of the present waterworks (Chicago Avenue and Tower Place) and finally to Graceland, where they now rest.

Unfortunately there exists no portrait of John Kinzie. The portrait of John H. Kinzie, taken from a miniature, and that of his wife, the author of Wau-Bun, are kindly furnished by their daughter, Mrs. Nellie Kinzie Gordon. There has also been copied an oil portrait of the last named lady herself, painted by Healy in 1857, when she was about to quit her native city for her home in Savannah, Georgia, which departure was a loss still remembered and regretted by her many Chicago friends and admirers; in other words by all of the Chicago of 1857 which survives to 1893.

Appendix D.

Figure 42. Mrs. Nellie (Kinzie) Gordon.

A fourth portrait of this honored branch of the pioneer stock is that of the son, John H. Kinzie, Jr., who died for his country in a manner which must endear his memory to every Union loving patriot. The following touching sketch of his life and death is contributed by a near relative of the brave young martyr.

John Harris Kinzie, Jr., was born in 1838. He was educated as a civil engineer at the Polytechnic Institute of Ann Arbor, Mich. He served in the navy during the war and met his tragic fate in 1862, while master's mate on the gun-boat Mound City, commanded by Admiral Davis.

While attacking a fort on the White River, a shot from the fort's battery penetrated the boiler of the Mound City. In the terrific explosion that followed, young Kinzie and more than ninety others were scalded and blown overboard.

The hospital boat of the fleet immediately set out to rescue the wounded men. As Kinzie struck out for the boat, his friend Augustus Taylor, of Cairo, called out to him to keep out of the range of the fort as the sharp-shooters were evidently picking off the wounded men in the water. This proved to be true; young Kinzie was shot through the legs and arras by minié balls as he was being lifted into the boat.

Figure 43. John Harris Kinzie, Jr.

He soon heard the shouts of his comrades; and turning to one of his friends, he said:

"We have taken the fort. I am ready to die now."

He sank rapidly and died the following morning, June 18, just as the sun was rising. He left a young wife barely eighteen years old, a daughter of Judge James, of Racine, Wisconsin, and his own little daughter was born three months after his death.

It was necessary to put a guard over the person of Colonel Fry (who was captured with the fort) to save him from being sacrificed to the indignation the men felt against him for having ordered his sharp-shooters to pick off the scalded men and shoot them in the water.

APPENDIX E.

WILLIAM WELLS AND REBEKAH WELLS HEALD

Gratitude to our first hero and martyr calls for a somewhat extended study of his life, and it will be found interesting enough to repay the attention.

Colonel Samuel Wells and his brother Captain William Wells were Kentuckians; the family being said to have come from Virginia. William, when twelve years old, was stolen by the Indians from the residence of Hon. Nathaniel Pope, where both brothers seem to have been living. He was adopted by Me-che-kan-nah-quah, or little Turtle, a chief of the Miamis, lived in his house and married his daughter Wa-nan-ga-peth, by whom he had several children, of whom the following left children:

Pe-me-zah-quah (Rebekah) married Captain Hackley, of Fort Wayne, leaving Ann and John Hackley, her children.

Ah-mah-qua-zah-quah (a "sweet breeze"—Mary) born at Fort Wayne May 10, 1800, married Judge James Wolcott March 8, 1821; died at Maumee City, (now South Toledo,) O., Feb. 19, 1834, leaving children as follows: William Wells Wolcott, Toledo; Mary Ann (Wolcott) Gilbert, South Toledo; Henry Clay Wolcott, South Toledo, and James Madison Wolcott, South Toledo.

Jane (Wells) Grigg, living at Peru, Indiana; has children.

Yelberton P. Wells, St. Louis, died leaving one child.

William fought on the side of the Indians in the campaign of 1790 and 1791, when they defeated the Americans under Generals Harmer and Saint Clair. The story of his reclamation, as told by Rebekah (Wells) Heald to her son Darius, and repeated by him to a stenographer, in my presence, in 1892, is quite romantic.

Rebekah was daughter of Samuel Wells, elder brother of William, and was therefore niece of the latter. She must have been born between 1780 and 1790. We learn from the story of her son, the Hon. Darius Heald, as follows:

> She was fond of telling the story of her life, and her children and her friends were never tired of listening to it. [Her son thinks he has heard her tell it a hundred times.] She would begin away back in her girlhood, spent in the country about Louisville, Kentucky, when her father, Colonel

Appendix E.   167

Samuel Wells, was living there; and tell how they all wanted uncle William Wells, whom they called their "Indian uncle," to leave the Indians who had stolen him in his boyhood, and come home and belong to his white relations. He hung back for years, and even at last, when he agreed to visit them, made the proviso that he should be allowed to bring along an Indian escort with him, so that he should not be compelled to stay with them if he did not want to.

Young Rebekah Wells was the one who had been chosen to go to the Indian council with her father, and persuade her uncle William to come and visit his old home; she, being a girl, very likely had more influence with him than any of the men could have had. William Wells was at that time living a wild Indian life, roaming up and down the Wabash river, and between the lakes and the Ohio. Probably the place where the battle of Tippicanoe was fought, in 1811, near the present site of La Fayette, Indiana, was pretty near the center of his regular stamping ground.

After much hesitation he consented to get together a party of braves, somewhere from seventy-five to a hundred, and visit his relatives. Little Turtle, whose daughter he had married, was along, very likely commanding the escort. They went down to the falls of the Ohio river, about opposite Louisville, and camped, while William Wells, with a picked band of twenty-five, crossed the river and met with his own people. Then the question arose as to whether he was the brother of Colonel Samuel Wells, and he asked to be taken to the place where he was said to have been captured, to see if he could remember the circumstances. When he reached there, he looked about and pointed in a certain direction and asked if there was a pond there; and they said: "Well, let's go and see." So they went in the direction indicated, and to be sure they saw the pond; and he said that he could remember that pond. Then he saw a younger brother present, whom he had accidentally wounded in the head as a child, and he said to his brother:

"Now if you are my brother there ought to be a mark on the back of your head, where I hit you with a stone one day;" and the brother held up his head, and William lifted the hair and found the scar, and he said: "Yes, I am your brother."

William was now convinced for the first time that he was the brother of Colonel Samuel Wells, but he went back with his Indian friends, his father-in-law, Little Turtle, and the rest, and it was not until sometime later that he told Little Turtle that, although he had fought for his Indian friends all his life, the time had now come when he was going home to fight for his own flesh and blood. It was under a big tree on the banks of the Miami that he had this talk, and he pointed to the sun and said: "Till the sun goes up in the middle of the sky we are friends. After that you can kill me if you want to." Still they always remained friends, and agreed that if in war, if one could find out on which side of the army the other was put, he would change positions so as not to be likely to meet the other in battle; and if one recognized the other while fighting, he would never aim to hit him. They also had the privilege of meeting and talking to each other, it being understood that nothing was to be said about the opposing numbers of their armies. They were not to act as spies but simply to meet each other as friends.

It was at about the time when General Wayne, "Mad Anthony," came into command that Wells left his red friends and began to serve on the side of his own flesh and blood. He was made captain of a company of scouts, and must have done good service, for, in 1798, he accompanied his father-in-law, Little Turtle, to Philadelphia, where the Indian (and probably Wells also) was presented to President Washington, and in 1803 we find him back at Chicago signing an Indian trader's license: "W. H. Harrison, Governor of Indian Territory, by William Wells, agent at Indian affairs." Little Turtle lived usually at Fort Wayne. Of him his friend John Johnston, of Piqua, Ohio, said:

> "He was a man of great wit, humor and vivacity, fond of the company of gentlemen and delighted in good eating. When I knew him he had two wives living with him under the same roof in the greatest harmony. This distinguished chief died at Fort Wayne of a confirmed case of gout, brought on by high living, and was buried with military honors by the troops of the United States."

He died July 14, 1812, and was buried on the west bank of the river at Fort Wayne. His portrait hangs on the walls of the War Department at Washington.

Appendix E.

In 1809 Captain Wells took his niece, Rebekah, with him to Fort Wayne on a visit. Captain Heald was then on duty at Fort Wayne, and it was doubtless there that the love-making took place which led to the marriage of the two young people in 1811.

The following interesting bits concerning Captain Wells are taken from a letter written by A. H. Edwards to Hon. John Wentworth (Fergus' Hist. Series No. 16), the remainder of which letter is given later in this volume. (See Appendix G.)

> Captain Wells, after being captured by the Indians when a boy, remained with them until the treaty with the Miamis. Somewhere about the year 1795 he was a chief and an adopted brother of the celebrated chief Little Turtle. Captain Wells signed the marriage certificate, as officiating magistrate, of my father and mother at Fort Wayne, June, 1805. The certificate is now in my possession.
>
> "Fort Wayne, 4th June.
> "I do hereby certify that I joined Dr. Abraham Edwards and Ruthy Hunt in the holy bonds of matrimony, on the third instant, according to the law.
> "Given under my Hand and Seal, the day and year above written.
> "William Wells, Esq."
>
> Captain Wells urged Major Heald not to leave the fort, as he did not like the way the Indians acted, and was well acquainted with all their movements as learned from his Indian allies, who deserted him the moment the firing commenced. Captain N. Heald's story is as I heard it from the mouth of one who saw it all, the girl and her mother, the one living in our family for many years, and the mother in Detroit. Their name was Cooper.
>
> Captain Wells, soon after leaving the Indians, was appointed interpreter at the request of General Wayne, and was with him in his campaign against the Indians as captain of a company of spies, and many thrilling accounts were given me of his daring and remarkable adventures as such, related by one who received them from his own lips, and in confirmation of one of his adventures pointed at an Indian present, and said: "That Indian," says he, "belongs to me, and sticks to me like a

brother," and then told how he captured him with his rifle on his shoulder. This Indian was the one who gave Mrs. Wells the first intimation of his death and then disappeared, supposed to have returned to his people.

Captain William Wells was acting Indian Agent and Justice of the Peace at Port Wayne at the time he married my father and mother, and was considered a remarkably brave and resolute man. I will give you a sketch of one of his feats as told me by my mother, who was present and witnessed it all. The Indians were collected at Fort Wayne on the way for the purpose of meeting the Miamis and other Indians in council. While camped there they invited the officers of the fort to come out and witness a grand dance, and other performances, previous to their departure for the Indian conference. Wells advised the commander of the fort not to go, as he did not like the actions of the Indians; but his advice was overruled, and all hands went out, including the officers' ladies. But the troops in the fort were on the alert, their guns were loaded and sentries were doubled, as it was in the evening. A very large tent was provided for the purpose of the grand dance. After many preliminary dances and talks, a large and powerful chief arose and commenced his dance around the ring, and made many flourishes with his tomahawk. Then he came up to Wells, who stood next my mother, and spoke in Indian and made demonstrations with his tomahawk that looked dangerous, and then took his seat. But no sooner than he did so Wells gave one of the most unearthly war-whoops she ever heard, and sprang up into the air as high as her head, and picked up the jaw bone of a horse or ox that lay nearby, and went around the ring in a more vigorous and artistic Indian style than had been seen that evening; and wound up by going up to the big Indian and flourishing his jaw-bone, and told him that he had killed more Indians than white men, and had killed one that looked just like him, and he believed it was his brother, only much better looking and a better brave than he was. The Indians were perfectly taken by surprise. Wells turned to the officers and told them to be going. He hurried them off to the fort, and had all hands on the alert during the night. When questioned as to his action and what he said, he replied that he had told the Indians what I have related. Then he enquired of those present if they did not see that the Indians standing on the opposite side of the tent had their rifles wrapped up in their blankets.

"If I had not done just as I had, and talked to that Indian as I did, we would all have been shot in five minutes; but my actions required a council, as their plans were, as they supposed, frustrated, and that the troops would be down on them at the first hostile move they made." He saw the game when he first went in, as his Indian training taught him, and he waited just for the demonstration that was made as the signal for action. Wells saw no time was to be lost, and made good his resolve, and the big Indian cowed under the demonstration of Wells. My mother said he looked as if he expected Wells to make an end of him for what he had said to Wells in his dance. "I had to meet bravado with bravado, and I think I beat," said Wells. You could see it in the countenances of all the Indians. The same advice given to Heald, if attended to, would have saved the massacre of Fort Dearborn.

A. H. Edwards.

James Madison Wolcott, grandson of Captain Wells (through Ah-mah-quah-zah-quah, who married Judge James Wolcott) wrote to Mr. Wentworth as follows:

We are proud of our Little Turtle [Indian] blood and of our Captain Wells blood. We try to keep up the customs of our ancestors, and dress occasionally in Indian costumes. We take no exception when people speak of our Indian parentage. We take pleasure in sending you the tomahawk which Captain William Wells had at the time of his death, and which was brought to his family by an Indian who was in the battle. We also have a dress-sword which was presented to him by General W. H. Harrison, and a great many books which he had; showing that even when he lived among the Indians, he was trying to improve himself. He did all he could to educate his children. Captain Wells, in the year of his death, sent to President Madison, at Little Turtle's request, the interpretation of the speech that that chief made to General W. H. Harrison, January 25, 1812.

Figure 44. Darius Heald, with Sword and Other Massacre Relics.

Captain Heald never got rid of the effect of his wound. The bullet remained embedded in his hip and doubtless is in his coffin. He resigned shortly after the war, and the family (in 1817) settled at Stockland, Missouri. The new name of the place, O'Fallon, recalls the fact that the well-known Colonel O'Fallon, of St. Louis, was an old friend of the family, and himself redeemed the things which the Indians had captured at the massacre (the same articles now cherished as relics of the historic event) and sent them to Colonel Samuel Wells at Louisville, where they arrived during the interval when all supposed that Nathan and Rebekah had perished with the members of the garrison and their fellow-sufferers.

Among the articles captured by the Indians and, after their transportation from Chicago to Peoria and from Peoria to Saint Louis, bought by Colonel O'Fallon and sent to the Falls of the Ohio (Louisville) to Samuel Wells, are the following, all of which were brought to Chicago by the Hon. Darius Heald, exhibited to his relatives (the family of Gen. A. L. Chetlain), and their friends, and here reproduced.

> Captain Heald's sword.
> A shawl-pin he wore which, when recovered, had been bent to serve as a nose-ring.
> Part of his uniform coat, which seems to have been divided among his captors.
> Six silver table-spoons and one soup-ladle, each marked "N. R. H.," doubtless the wedding-present made by Colonel Samuel Wells to Nathan and Rebekah Heald.
> A hair brooch marked "S. W.," supposed to contain the hair of Samuel Wells.
> A finger-ring marked "R. W." (Probably one of the girlish treasures of Rebekah Wells.)
> A fine tortoise-shell comb, cut somewhat in the shape of an eagle's beak and having silver ornaments representing the bird's eye, nostril, etc.

Mr. Wentworth further says:

> In the biographical sketches of the members of the Corinthian Lodge of Masons, at Concord, Mass., I find the following:

Nathan Heald, initiated in 1797, died at Stockland (now O'Fallon) in St. Charles County, Missouri, where he had resided some years, in 1832, aged 57 years. He was born in Ipswich, N. H., September 29, 1775, was the third sou of Colonel Thomas and Sybel (Adams) Heald and in early life joined the U. S. Army. Mrs. Maria (Heald) Edwards, of this city, born at Ipswich, N. H, in 1803, mother of Mrs. General Chetlain, was the eldest child of his brother, Hon. Thomas Heald, one of the Associate Judges of the Supreme Court of Alabama. (Fergus' Hist. Series No. 16.)

A considerable part of Captain Heald's first report of the massacre appears in our old friend Niles' Weekly Register, Nov. 7, 1812. (I have quoted it, to a great extent, in connection with the story of the event.)

Extract of a letter from Captain Heald, late commandant at Fort Chicago, dated at Pittsburg, October 23, 1812:

> On the 9th of August, I received orders from General Hull to evacuate the post and proceed with my command to Detroit, by land, leaving it at my discretion to dispose of the public property as I thought proper. The neighboring Indians got the information as soon as I did, and came in from all quarters to receive goods in the factory-store, which they understood were to be given to them. On the 13th, Captain Wells, of Fort Wayne, arrived with about thirty Miamis, for the purpose of escorting us in, by request of General Hull. On the 14th I delivered to the Indians all the goods of the factory-store, and a considerable quantity of provisions which we could not take with us. The surplus arms and ammunition I thought proper to destroy, fearing they would make bad use of it, if put in their possession. I also destroyed all liquor on hand soon after they began to collect.
>
> The collection was unusually large for that place, but they conducted with the strictest propriety until after I left the fort. On the 15th, at 9 A. M., we commenced our march. A part of the Miamis were detached in front, the remainder in our rear, as guards, under the direction of Captain Wells. The situation of the country rendered it necessary for us to take the beach, with the lake on our left and a high sand-bank on our right at about one hundred yards distance. We had proceeded about a mile and a half when it was discovered that the Indians were prepared to attack us from behind the bank. I immediately marched up, with the company, to the top

of the bank, when the action commenced; after firing one round we charged, and the Indians gave way in front and joined those on our flanks. In about fifteen minutes they got possession of all our horses, provisions, and baggage of every description, and, finding the Miamis did not assist us, I drew off the men I had left and took possession of a small elevation in the open prairie, out of shot of the bank or any other cover. The Indians did not follow me but assembled in a body on the top of the bank, and after some private consultation among themselves, made signs for me to approach them. I advanced toward them alone and was met by one of the Pottowatomie chiefs called Black-bird, with an interpreter. After shaking hands, he requested me to surrender, promising to spare the lives of all the prisoners. On a few moments consideration I concluded it would be most prudent to comply with his request, although I did not put entire confidence in his promise. After delivering up our arms we were taken back to their encampment near the fort, and distributed among the different tribes.

The next morning they set fire to the fort and left the place, taking the prisoners with them. Their number of warriors was between four and five hundred, mostly from the Pottowatomie nation, and their loss, from the best information I could get, was about fifteen. Our strength was about fifty-four regulars and twelve militia, out of which twenty-six regulars and all the militia were killed in the action, with two women and twelve children. Ensign George Ronan and Dr. Isaac Van Voorhis of my company, with Captain Wells of Fort Wayne, to my great sorrow, are numbered among the dead. Lieutenant Linai T. Helm, with twenty-five non-commissioned officers and privates and eleven women and children, were prisoners when we separated.

Mrs. Heald and myself were taken to the mouth of the river St. Joseph, and, being both badly wounded, were permitted to reside with Mr. Burnett, an Indian trader. In a few days after our arrival there, the Indians went off to take Fort Wayne, and in their absence I engaged a Frenchman to take us to Michilimackinac by water, where I gave myself up as a prisoner of war, with one of my sergeants. The commanding officer, Captain Roberts, offered me every assistance in his power to render our situation comfortable while we remained there, and to enable us to proceed on our journey.

To him I gave my parole of honor, and came to Detroit and reported myself to Colonel Proctor, who gave us a passage to Buffalo, from that place I came by way of Presque-Isle, and arrived here yesterday.

Nathan Heald.

The following letter from Captain Heald, written three years after taking up his residence in Missouri, speaks for itself:

St. Charles, Missouri Territory May 18th, 1820.

Sir:—I had the honor of receiving your letter of the 30th of March, a few days since. The garrison at Chicago commanded by me at the time Detroit was surrendered by General Hull, were every man paid up to the 30th of June, 1812, inclusive, officers' subsistence and forage included.

The last payment embraced nine months, and was made by myself as the agent of Mr. Eastman, but I cannot say what the amount was. Every paper relative to that transaction was soon after lost. I am, however, confident that there was no deposit with me to pay the garrison for the three months subsequent to the 30th of June, 1812.

The receipt-rolls which I had taken from Mr. Eastman, together with the balance of money in my hands, fell into the hands of the Indians on the 15th of August, 1812, when the troops under my command were defeated near Chicago; what became of them afterwards I know not. I have no papers in my possession relative to that garrison, excepting one muster-roll for the month of May, 1812. By it I find that the garrison there consisted of one captain, one 2nd lieutenant, one ensign, one surgeon's mate, four sergeants, two corporals, four musicians and forty-one privates. I cannot determine what the strength of the garrison was at any other time during the years 1811 and 1812, but it was on the decline. Monthly returns were regularly submitted to the Adjutant and Inspector-General's office, at Washington City, which, I suppose, can be found at any time.

I am respectfully sir, your most obedient servant,
Nathan Heald.

APPENDIX F.

THE BONES OF JOHN LALIME.—SUBSTANCE OF A PAPER READ BY JOSEPH KIRKL AND BEFORE THE CHICAGO HISTORICAL SOCIETY, ON THE OCCASION OF THE PRESENTATION TO THE SOCIETY OF CERTAIN HUMAN RELICS, JULY 21, 1891

180 Joseph Kirkland

Some ominous threatenings were heard at old Ft. Dearborn before the bursting of the storm of August 15, 1812. Among them was the killing of the interpreter for the government, John Lalime.

John Kinzie arrived at Fort Dearborn in 1804, and with his family occupied a house built of squared logs, which, up to about 1840, stood where the corner of Cass and Kinzie streets now is. He was an Indian-trader, furnishing what the savages desired and taking furs in exchange. The government also had an Indian agent, or trader, there.

Various circumstances tend to show that before 1812 considerable rivalry existed between the government fur-trading agency and the civilian dealers. The former had certain advantages in the cheapness of purchase and transportation, but were restricted as to selling liquor. The latter were nominally under the same restriction, but practically free, and the Indians, like other dipsomaniacs, hated every man who tried to restrain their drinking. The short-sighted savages mistook their friends for their enemies, their enemies for their friends. They loved the poison and the poisoner.

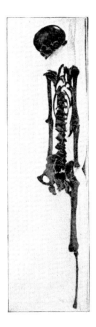

Figure 46. Remains unearthed April 26th and presented to the Historical Society July 27, 1891.

Appendix F.

Mrs. Kinzie, in Wau-Bun, says that there were two factions in the garrison, the Kinzies sympathizing with the opposition. Also that, though the garrison was massacred, no Kinzie was injured, the immunity extending even to Lieutenant Linai T. Helm, who had married Mr. Kinzie's step-daughter. Also that while the fort was burned, the Kinzie mansion was left untouched, and remained standing up to within the memory of living men.

For several years before 1812, John Lalime, a Frenchman, had been the government's salaried interpreter at Fort Dearborn. The earliest mention of the name occurs in a letter written from St. Joseph by William Burnett to his Detroit correspondent, which begins with the words: "When Mr. Lalime was in Detroit last you was pleased to tell him that if I should want anything at your house, it should be at my service." The next intelligence about him is in two letters he wrote concerning Indian matters. The first was to Wm. Clark, Governor of Missouri, and reads as follows:

> Chicago, 26th May, 1811.
> Sir—An Indian from the Peorias passed here yesterday and has given me information that the Indians about that place have been about the settlements of Kaskasia and Vincennes and have stolen from fifteen to twenty horses. It appears by the information given me that the principal actors are two brothers of the wife of Main Foe. He is residing on the Peoria, or a little above it, at a place they call "Prairie du Corbeau." By the express going to Fort Wayne I will communicate this to the agent. I presume, sir, that you will communicate this to the Governor of Kaskasia and General Harrison. I am sir, with respect,
> Y'r h'ble serv't,
> J. Lalime.

The second letter is the one mentioned in the first. It is written to John Johnson, United States factor at Fort Wayne, dated July 7th, 1811, and reads as follows:

> Since my last to you we have news of other depredations and murders committed about the settlement of Cahokia. The first news we

received was that the brother-in-law of Main Poc went down and stole a number of horses. Second, another party went down, stole some horses, killed a man and took off a young woman, but they being pursued were obliged to leave her to save themselves. Third, they have been there and killed and destroyed a whole family. The cause of it in part is from the Little Chief that came last fall to see Governor Harrison under the feigned name of Wapepa. He told the Indians that he had told the governor that the Americans were settling on their lands, and asked him what should be done with them. He told the Indians that the Governor had told him they were bad people.

We observe that the Peoria chief, Main Poc, is mentioned as blameworthy for these wrongs. It may be interesting to know Main Poc's side of the question. Said he:

You astonish me with your talk! Whenever you do wrong there is nothing said or done; but when we do anything you immediately take us and tie us by the neck with a rope. You say, what will become of our women and children if there is war? On the other hand, what will become of your women and children? It is best to avoid war.

Lalime's letters show that he was a man of ability and education. We also guess, from a clause in Article III of the treaty of 1821, that Lalime lived after the manner of those days, and left at least one half-breed child. The clause reserves a half-section of land for "John B. Lalime, son of Noke-no-qua."

Miss Noke-no-qua is not otherwise known to history.

The next knowledge we have of Lalime relates to his violent death in the spring of 1812, about five months before the massacre, at a point on the south bank of the river within a stone's throw of where is now the south end of Rush Street bridge.

Peter Hagner, Esq., 3rd Auditor's Office, Treasury Department, Washington City.

This brings up to the mind of every officer the terrors of the "Auditors of the Treasury." Not victory or defeat, not wounds or even death—nay, not old Time himself can clear a soldier from the terrible ordeal of the "Accounting Department." Poor Heald had evidently been asked: "Where is the money which was in your hands before the savages surrounded you, slaughtered your troops, wounded yourself and your wife, massacred the civilians under your care, tortured to death your wounded and burned your fort?" At the same time the ordnance bureau doubtless asked what had become of the arms, ammunition, accoutrements and cooking utensils; the commissary bureau asked after the stores and the quartermaster's bureau after the equippage. Scores of thousands of volunteer officers in the Union war found to their cost that their fighting was the only thing which the War Department kept no record of; that their account-keeping and reporting was what must be most carefully looked after if they would free themselves, their heirs, executors and assigns, from imperishable obligations. For the government knows no "statute of limitations"—takes no account of the lapse of time any more than does Nature in her operations. "Contra regem tempus non occurret."

Yet, paradoxical as it may seem, this is right. If all men were honest, "red tape" could be done away with; but as men are, individual accountability is indispensable. Without it, the army might fall into negligence leading to corruption, instead of being, as it is, the very example of administrational honor and probity.

It so happens that the death of Mrs. Maria (Heald) Edwards, niece of Captain Nathan Heald and mother of Mrs. General Chetlain, is announced after the above matter had been put in print. She died on May 6, 1893, at the residence of General Chetlain, in this city, at the ripe age of ninety years.

It stirs the heart to think that, almost up to this very day, there was living among us so near a relative to the gallant and unfortunate captain; a woman who was a girl nine years old when her uncle passed through the direful ordeal.

Figure 45. Massacre Tree and Part of Pullman House.

Appendix F.

Figure 47. Gurdon Saltonstall Hubbard. (Last picture taken of him.)

In a letter written by the lamented Gurdon Hubbard to John Wentworth, June 25th, 1881, we read:

> As regards the unfortunate killing of Mr. Lalime by Mr. John Kinzie, I have heard the account of it related by Mrs. Kinzie and her daughter, Mrs. Helm. Mr. Kinzie never, in my hearing, alluded to or spoke of it. He deeply regretted the act. Knowing his aversion to conversing on the subject, I never spoke to him about it.
>
> Mrs. Kinzie said that her husband and Lalime had for several years been on unfriendly terms, and had had frequent altercations; that at the time of the encounter Mr. Kinzie had crossed the river alone, in a canoe,

going to the fort, and that Lalime met him outside the garrison and shot him, the ball cutting the side of his neck. She supposed that Lalime saw her husband crossing, and taking his pistol went through the gate purposely to meet him. Mr. Kinzie, closing with Lalime, stabbed him and returned to the house covered with blood. He told his wife what he had done, that he feared he had killed Lalime, and probably a squad would be sent for him and that he must hide. She, in haste, took bandages and with him retreated to the woods, where as soon as possible she dressed his wounds, returning just in time to meet an officer with a squad with orders to seize her husband. He could not be found. For several days he was hid in the bush and cared for by his wife.

Lalime was, I understand, an educated man, and quite a favorite with the officers, who were greatly excited. They decided he should be buried near Kinzie's house, in plain view from his front door and piazza. The grave was enclosed in a picket fence, which Mr. Kinzie, in his lifetime, kept in perfect order. My impression has ever been that Mr. Kinzie acted, as he told his wife, in self-defence. This is borne out by the fact that, after a full investigation by the officers, whose friend the deceased was, they acquitted Mr. Kinzie, who then returned to his family.

In some of these details I may be in error, but the fact has always been firm in my mind that Lalime made the attack, provoking the killing, in self-defence. Mr. Kinzie deeply regretted the result, and avoided any reference to it.

Yours,
G. S. Hubbard.

Mr. Hubbard does not say he remembers having seen the grave. He did not come to Chicago to live until 1836. Judge Blodgett, as we shall see hereafter, describes its position as not on the river bank, but back in the timber.

A somewhat different account of the affair was given by Mrs. Porthier (Victoire Mirandeau,) and printed in Captain Andreas' *History of Chicago*, Vol. II, page 105.

My sister Madeline and I saw the fight between John Kinzie and Lalime, when Lalime was killed. It was sunset, when they used to shut the gates of the fort. Kinzie and Lalime came out together, and soon we heard Lieutenant Helm call out for Mr. Kinzie to look out for Lalime, as he had a pistol. Quick we saw the men come together. We heard the pistol go off and saw the smoke. Then they fell down together. I don't know as Lalime got up at all, but Kinzie got home pretty quick. Blood was running from his shoulder, where Lalime had shot him. In the night he packed up some things and my father took him to Milwaukee, where he stayed until his shoulder got well and he found he would not be troubled if he came back. You see, Kinzie wasn't to blame at all. He didn't have any pistol nor knife—nothing. After Lalime shot him and Kinzie got his arms around him, he (Lalime) pulled out his dirk, and as they fell he was stabbed with his own knife. That is what they all said. I didn't see the knife at all. I don't remember where Lalime was buried. I don't think his grave was very near Kinzie's house. I don't remember that Mr. Kinzie ever took care of the grave. That is all I know about it. I don't know what the quarrel was about. It was an old one—business, I guess.

This bears all the thumb-marks of truth. It comes at first hand from a disinterested eye-witness. Even if we suppose Mrs. Kinzie to have seen the affray, which she does not say, it was doubtless from the opposite side of the river, while Victoire and her sister were in the fort itself. No other account, direct from an eye-witness, has ever been published.

Now, without pretending to certainty, it strikes me as probable that up to this time Kinzie stood on the Indian side of the irrepressible conflict between white men and red men, while the army and Lalime took the other. Mrs. Helm's narrative in Wau-Bun is decidedly hostile to the good sense of the commandant of the fort, and even to the courage of some of his faithful subordinates, while obviously friendly to the mutinous element in his command. Therefore it seems to me quite likely that Lalime's crazy attack on Kinzie was not entirely disconnected with that irrepressible conflict, that this long-standing quarrel had more than appears on the surface to do with the admitted success of Kinzie's trade and the well-known unprofitableness of the business carried on by the government agency.

On April 29th, 1891, there was unearthed at the southwest corner of Cass and Illinois streets, a skeleton. Workmen were digging a cellar there for a large new building, and were startled by having the shovel stopped by a skull, wherein its edge made a slight abrasion. Further examination brought to light some spinal vertebrae, some fragments of ribs, some remains of shoulder-blades and pelvis-bones, some bones of the upper and lower arms and the hip-bones, besides two bones of the lower part of one leg; also fragments, nearly crumbled away, of a rude pine coffin. The rumor of the discovery spread through the neighborhood, and luckily reached the ears of Mr. Scott Fergus, son of the veteran printer, Robert Fergus, whose establishment stands within ten feet of the place where these relics of mortality had so long lain unnoticed.

Mr. Fergus at once tried to save and collect the bones, and finding some disposition on the part of the laborers to disregard his requests, he rang for the police-patrol wagon, which bundled the little lot into a soap-box and carried them to the East Chicago Avenue station.

I was out of town at this time and did not hear of the interesting occurrence until Mr. Fergus told me of it upon my return, about a month later. I then went to the station, only to learn that the bones, being unclaimed, had been sent in the patrol-wagon to the morgue at the County Hospital, on the West Side. However, on looking up the officer who carried them over, he freely and kindly offered to try to reclaim them, and have them delivered to the Historical Society. The morgue officials, after a few days, at a merely nominal expense, complied with the request, and they are now here. Was this, *is* this the skeleton of John Lalime?

The place where the bones were found is within a stone's throw of the exact spot indicated by Gurdon Hubbard as the place where the picket fence marked the grave, "two hundred yards west of the Kinzie house."

Dr. Arthur B. Hosmer, and Dr. Otto Freer, who have examined the relics independently of each other, and assisted me in arranging them in human semblance, consider them to be the skeleton of a slender white man, about five feet and four inches in height.

The color, consistency and general conditions indicate that they had lain in the ground (dry sand) for a very long time, reaching probably or possibly the seventy-nine years which have elapsed since Lalime's death.

Now, admitting their expert judgment to be correct, this man died not far from 1812. At that time there had not and never had been in all these parts more than some fifty to one hundred white men, nearly all of whom were soldiers, living in the fort and subject to burial in the fort burying-ground, adjoining the present site of Michigan Avenue and Randolph street. At a later date, say fifty years ago, isolated burials were not uncommon, but even then they could scarcely have occurred in so public a spot as the north bank cf the river, close to the docks and warehouses which had been by that time built there.

John C. Haines, Fernando Jones and others remember perfectly the existence of that lonely little fenced enclosure, and even that it was said to mark the resting-place of a man killed in a fight. They and all others agree that no other burials were made thereabouts, so far as known. Another point, favorable or otherwise to this identification, is the fact that the place where the skeleton was found is the lot whereon stood the first St. James Church, and that the attendants there, as I was informed by one of them, Mr. Ezra McCagg, never heard of any burial as having taken place in the church-yard.

On the other hand, Mr. Hubbard designates "the river bank" as the place of burial, and the memory of Mr. Fernando Jones is to the effect that the fenced enclosure was nearer to the place of Rush Street bridge than is the spot of finding.

But in contradiction to this view. Judge Blodgett tells me that he was here in 1831 and 1832, which was several years before either Mr. Jones or Mr. Haines, and before Mr. Hubbard came here to live, he being then trading at Danville. The Judge adds that with the Beaubien and Laframboise boys he paddled canoes on the creek, played in the old Kinzie log-house and wandered all about the numerous paths that ran along the river bank, and back into the thick, tangled underbrush which filled the woods, covering almost all the North Side west of the shore sand-hills. He says that one path over which they traveled back and forth ran from the old house west to the forks of the river, passing north of the old Agency house—"Cobweb Castle"—which stood near the northeast corner of Kinzie and State Streets. Also that from that path behind Cobweb Castle the boys pointed further north to where they said there was a grave where the man was buried whom John Kinzie had killed, but they never went out to that spot, and so far as he remembered he never saw the grave. A kind of awe kept him quite clear of that place. All he knows is that it was somewhere out in the brush behind the Agency house.

This seems to locate the grave as nearly as possible at the corner of Illinois and Cass streets, where these relics were found. Fernando Jones suggests that even if the grave was originally elsewhere, the remains might have got into the church lot in this way: In 1832 Robert Kinzie entered and subdivided Kinzie's Addition, bounded by Chicago Avenue on the north, the lake on the east, Kinzie Street on the south and State Street on the west, and gradually he and his brother John sold the lots. In 1835 they gave the St. James Society the two lots where the church was built and wherein this skeleton was found. What more likely than that on selling the lot whereon the original interment took place (supposing it to be other than where the bones were unearthed) the sellers were compelled, either by the buyer's stipulation or their own sense of duty to their father's manifest wishes, to find a new place for the coffin of poor Lalime, and thereupon selected the spare room in the new church-yard?

It is worthy of note, that as, with the skeleton, were found the remains of a coffin—a single bit of pine board, showing the well-known "shoulder angle," though decayed so that only a crumbling strip half an inch thick was left—this could not have been a secret interment, made to conceal the death of a man. It would seem utterly improbable that two men's bodies should have been coffined and buried within the little space of ground, in the few years of time pointed out by all these circumstances. We learn that Lalime was so buried; also that, so far as known, all other excavations thereabouts have failed to expose his remains; also that these relics have now come to light. Everyone must draw his own conclusion. I have drawn mine. If it be erroneous, this exploitation of the subject will be likely to bring out the truth.

Appendix F. 189

LETTER FROM FERNANDO JONES

Chicago, July 20th, 1891.

Joseph Kirkland, Esquire:

Dear Sir—In answer to your inquiry as to any incidents coming to my knowledge as to the grave of John Lalime, who was buried near the mouth of the Chicago River in the year 1812, I furnish the following statement:

When I arrived in Chicago, on my sixteenth birthday, May 26th, 1835, I landed on the north side of the present river, near its mouth, very near to the old John Kinzie homestead. I was escorted to the historic Cobweb Castle and the Dearborn Street bridge by the children of an old friend of my father's, Samuel Jackson, who was employed upon the north pier harbor work, and who had been an old neighbor in Buffalo, New York, where he had also been employed upon the government harbor. The little boy, Ezra, and the girl, Abigail, pointed out a grave situated a little to the north of our path and several hundred feet west of the Kinzie house. The grave was surrounded by a neat white picket fence. I passed it many times afterward, during that and the succeeding summer, and often visited it with children about my own age. The history of this lonely grave, as detailed by them, gave it a peculiar fascination to me, and to them, and to others who saw it. I recall now, after an interval of more than half a century, a number of persons who visited this grave with me, among whom were the Indian wife of Captain Jamison; the wife of Lieut. Thompson, a half-breed woman; Virginia Baxley, daughter of Captain Baxley, of the fort; Pierre Laframboise, son of a chief and interpreter; Alexander Beaubien, son of a trader, and John C. Haines, who was also a clerk near me on South Water Street.

The tradition in regard to this grave was that it was the last resting-place of a Frenchman named Lalime, who was government interpreter at the fort, and who was killed in an encounter with the old Indian-trader, John Kinzie. It was said that the officers of the garrison had the body buried in sight of Mr. Kinzie's house in resentment for his murder. But it seems that old Mr. Kinzie took the sting from this reproach by carefully tending the spot during his lifetime, and his son, John H. Kinzie, continued the same care over it.

Soon after the erection of St. James Episcopal Church, about the year 1838, a grave was noticed on the north side of the lot and in the rear of the church, which was situated on the southwest corner of Cass and Illinois Streets, and opposite the new house of John H. Kinzie. The lot upon which the Frenchman was buried had been sold by Mr. John H. Kinzie, and was built upon, and Mr. Kinzie had given the lot upon the corner for the church. Mr. Alonzo C. Wood, the builder of the church, who still survives, informs me that the grave appeared there mysteriously, and his remembrance is that the Rev. Mr. Hallam, the priest in charge, informed him that the remains were placed there by the direction of Mr. Kinzie, or Mrs. Kinzie, but he has no further distinct recollection in regard to it. I, myself, never mentioned the subject to Mr. John H. Kinzie, but remember a conversation with his brother, Robert A. Kinzie, U. S. Paymaster, in which he expressed satisfaction that his brother had taken care of the bones of poor Lalime. It was understood by the few conversant with the history of Lalime's death that both the elder Kinzie and his son, John H., were averse to speaking of the matter, but "Bob" was very like an Indian, and not at all reticent on the question, and that the legend among those who took any interest in the matter has always been that this solitary grave in the church-yard was the grave of the "little Frenchman" who was first buried near the spot. Under the circumstances, it is not strange that the removal should have been quietly made, and I have little doubt in my own mind that the tradition is correct.

Very sincerely yours,
Fernando Jones.

LETTER FROM THE HON. J. C. HAINES

Chicago, 15 July, 1891.
Major J. Kirkland:
Without very definite recollection as to just where the grave of John Lalime stood in 1835, when I came to Chicago, I can say that I knew of its existence and have an impression it stood in St. James' Church lot, corner of Cass and Michigan Streets.
John C. Haines.

Appendix F.

Dr. Hosmer's Letter

108 Pine Street, Chicago,
July 11, 1893.

The bones shown me at this date at the Chicago Historical Society, constitute the major portion of a human skeleton—that of an adult white male of slender build and about five feet four to five inches in height. There is evidence of a partial or complete fracture of the left femur, at some time in his life, thoroughly repaired and with some permanent thickening of the bone.

Judging by the color, weight and rotten condition of the bones, I believe that they have been in the ground (supposing it to be sandy and above water-level) at least sixty (60) but not to exceed one hundred (100) years.

A. B. Hosmer, M. D.

Dr. Freer's Letter

The skeleton shown me by Mr. Joseph Kirkland is without doubt of great age and resembles in appearance fragments of others that have lain for many years in sandy soil. All animal matter has departed from the bones, leaving them very light and consisting of the mineral portions alone.

The type of skeleton is that of a man of moderate stature and light build. The skull is that of a white man and of great symmetry. The lower jaw is missing, but the upper perfect, barring loss of all teeth but one. The presence of the third molar's sockets speaks for the complete maturity of the man. It is impossible exactly to estimate the exact time that the skeleton has been in the ground, but its appearance would tally well with the eighty years it is supposed to have lain there.

Dr. O. T. Freer.
July 20th, 1891.

Figure 48. The Late Calumet Club-House.

APPENDIX G.

IMPORTANT REMINISCENCES OF AN OLD SETTLER (A. H. EDWARDS).—[FROM "FORT DEARBORN"; FERGUS' HISTORICAL SERIES, NO. 16.]

Sheboygan (Wis.), May 24th, 1891.
Hon. John Wentworth:

Dear Sir—I have had the pleasure of reading your account and also the remarks of others in regard to Chicago and Illinois history. I am acquainted with some facts derived from conversation with one who was there, and witnessed the fight and killing of many of those who lost their lives on that memorable day. She was a daughter of one of the soldiers, and was one of the children who, with her mother and sisters, occupied the wagons, or conveyances that was to convey them from the fort. She told me she saw her father when he fell, and also many others. She, with her mother and sisters, were taken prisoners among the Indians for nearly two years, and were finally taken to Mackinac and sold to the traders and sent to Detroit. On our arrival in Detroit, in 1816, after the war, this girl was taken into our family, and was then about thirteen years old, and had been scalped. She said a young Indian came to the wagon where she was and grabbed her by the hair and pulled her out of the wagon, and she fought him the best she knew how, scratching and biting, till finally he threw her down and scalped her. She was so frightened she was not aware of it until the blood ran down her face. An old squaw interfered and prevented her from being tomahawked by the Indian, she going with the squaw to her wigwam, and was taken care of and her head cured. This squaw was one that often came to their house. The bare spot on the top of the head was about the size of a silver dollar. She saw Captain Wells killed, and told the same story as related in your pamphlet.

My father was well acquainted with Captain Wells; was stationed with him at Fort Wayne, Indiana, where I was born, in 1807, and he was surgeon of the post. My mother was a daughter of Col. Thomas Hunt of the Fifth Infantry.

I think there must be a mistake as to the year the Kinzies returned to Chicago. My father and family arrived in Detroit in June, 1816; the Kinzies were there then, and I was schoolmate of John, Robert, Ellen and Maria during that year, and I think they returned to Chicago in 1817. Mr. Kinzie went in the fall of 1816, and the family in the spring of 1817.

I was in Chicago in 1832 in the Black Hawk War time, as First Lieutenant of cavalry, from Michigan. The regiment was commanded by General Hart L. Stewart, now living in Chicago.

During the Black Hawk War, and when in Chicago, we heard of the killing of the Hall family and the carrying off of the two girls. Our company camped that night at the mouth of the Little Calumet, and next morning went into Chicago, and the fort was occupied by women and children of the surrounding country.

Then I saw for the last time my schoolmate, R. A. Kinzie. My brother. Col. L. A. H. Edwards, was in command of the fort after we left, and had a Cass County regiment of military from Michigan. We met him on our return at Door Prairie. He remained there until the arrival of Major Whistler, in June, 1832; he retired from the fort before the landing of any of the U. S. troops, on account of cholera being among them, and he wished to avoid any contact with them on that account. His command camped on the prairie, about a mile from the fort, and remained only a day or two. Fearing the cholera might get among his men, he left for home, as he saw they were not needed any longer, and was so informed by Major Whistler.

Captain Anderson, Ensign Wallace and myself camped under the hospitable roof of General Beaubien, on the bank of the lake, not very far

Appendix G. 195

from the fort, who had kept the only house there. Mark Beaubien Jr. went into Chicago with us, he having joined us at Niles, on his way home from school. He was the son of the one called the fiddler.

Our family lived in Detroit and were well acquainted with the Whistlers. My father, Major Edwards, was in Detroit at the surrender of Hull, as Surgeon-General of the Northwestern Army. He went from Ohio, and arriving in Detroit, received his appointment. Our family was then living in Dayton, Ohio. At the close of the war he resigned, and in 1816 removed to Detroit and was appointed sutler to all Northwestern posts—Fort Gratiot, Mackinac, Green Bay [Fort Howard], and Chicago [Fort Dearborn]—his books, now in my possession, showing his dealings with each of these stores, and all the officers mentioned in your paper.

It is pleasant to note that at the disastrous fire at the Calumet Club, which occurred while these pages were preparing, the Beaubien fiddle and the Wells hatchet were saved.

Sheboygan (Wis.), Jan. 10, 1881.

Your letter of the 5th came to hand to-day. The person I named as being present at the massacre, was a daughter of Cooper,[49] one of the soldiers who was killed in the fight. Her account, as given to me, as also her mother's, was that as soon as all the soldiers were disposed of, the Indians made a rush for the wagons, where the women and children were. Her mother, and sister younger than herself, were taken from the wagon and carried away. A young Indian boy about fourteen or fifteen years old dragged her by the hair out of the wagon, and she bit and scratched him so badly that he finally scalped her and would have killed her if an old squaw had not prevented him. I think she married a man by the name of Farnum and lived many years in Detroit. Her mother died there about the year 1832. The sisters were living in Detroit in 1828. I have since heard they were living in Mackinac. I do not know the first name of Cooper. He was killed and the girl said she saw her father's scalp in the hands of an Indian afterward. He had sandy hair. I think she said they were Scotch. Isabella had children. The girl said she saw Wells when he fell from his

---

[49] "John Cooper, Surgeon's Mate," is found in the muster-roll. He also signed the certificate to the roll.

horse, and that his face was painted. What became of her sister I do not know, as I left Detroit in 1823, but my father and mother remained there until 1828. You will receive with this a statement written by my father regarding himself, a short time before his death, which occurred in October, 1860, at Kalamazoo, Mich., where he had resided for many years. The statement will give you all the information in regard to himself as well as who my mother was. Her father, Thomas Hunt, was appointed a surgeon in the army directly after the battle of Bunker Hill, where he was brought into notice by an act of gallantry, then only a boy of fifteen. He remained in the army until his death, in 1808, in command of his regiment, at Bellefontaine, Missouri. His sons and grandsons have been representatives in the army ever since. Captain Thomas Hunt, mentioned in your letter, was a son, and the present General Henry J. Hunt, of the Artillery, and General Lewis C. Hunt, commanding the Fourth Infantry, grandsons, whose father (my mother's brother) was Captain Samuel W. Hunt of the army.

My grandfather, Thomas Hunt, was a captain under Lafayette, and was wounded at Yorktown in storming a redoubt of the British. Afterward he was with General Anthony Wayne in his campaign against the Indians, and was left in command of Fort Wayne as its first commander after the subjection of the Indians.

A. H. Edwards.

Figure 49. The Sauganash (1833).

For other extracts from this interesting paper see Appendix E—"The Wells and Heald families."

APPENDIX H.

BILLY CALDWELL, THE SAUGANASH

The Sauganash had qualities, good and bad, appertaining to each of his parent races. He had fighting courage and coolness in danger, he had physical endurance, he had personal faithfulness to personal friends, he had a love of strong drink. There is now (1893) in this city, an account-book kept which was at a Chicago grocery store in the thirties, wherein appear many charges reading: "One quart whisky to B. Caldwell." The book is in possession of Julian Rumsey, Esq., a relative of Mrs. Juliette (Magill) Kinzie, author of "Wau-Bun."

When the inevitable separation came, and the Indians, after a grand farewell war-dance (August 18, 1835),[50] departed on their migration toward the setting sun, Caldwell went with them, and died September 28, 1841, at Council Bluffs, Iowa. His old friend Mark Beaubien, had named after him the first and most noted of Chicago's real hotels, the "Sauganash," lovingly remembered by many of the "first families."

Letter written by the Sauganash [Billy Caldwell] and Shabonee [Chambly].

---

[50] See Appendix I.

Figure 50. Me-Tee-A; A Signer of the Treaty of 1821.

Council Bluffs, March 23rd, 1840. *To General Harrison's Friends:*

The other day several newspapers were brought to us; and peeping over them, to our astonishment we found that the hero of the late war was called a coward. This would have surprised the tall braves, Tecumseh, of the Shawnees, and Round Head and Walk-in-the-water of the late Tomahawkees. The first time we got acquainted with General Harrison, it was at the council fires of the late Old Tempest, General Wayne, on the headquarters of the Wabash at Greenville, 1796. From that time till 1811 we had many friendly smokes with him; but from 1812 we changed our tobacco smoke into powder smoke. Then we found that General Harrison was a brave warrior and humane to his prisoners, as reported to us by two of Tecumseh's young men, who were taken in the fleet with Captain Barclay on the 10th of September, 1813, and on the Thames, where he routed both the red-men and the British, and where he showed his courage and his humanity to his prisoners, both white and red. See report of Adams Brown and family, taken on the morning of the battle, October 5th, 1813. We are the only two surviving of that day in this country. We hope the good white men will protect the name of General Harrison. We remain your friends forever.

Chamblee [Shabonee], Aid to Tecumseh.

APPENDIX I.

FAREWELL WAR-DANCE OF THE INDIANS

Early in 1833 Indians to the number of five thousand or more, assembled at Chicago, around the fort, the village, the rivers and the portage, to treat for the sale of their entire remaining possessions in Illinois and Wisconsin. John Joseph Latrobe, in his "Rambles in North America," gives the following realistic sketch of the state of things hereabouts just sixty years ago:

> A mushroom town on the verge of a level country, crowded to its utmost capacity and beyond, a surrounding cloud of Indians encamped on the prairie, beneath the shelter of the woods, on the river-side or by the low sand-hills along the lake, companies of old warriers under every bush, smoking, arguing, palavering, pow-wowing, with no apparent prospect of agreement.

The negotiations dragged on for weeks and months, for the Indians were slow to put an end to their jollification, an occasion when they were the guests of the Government, and fared sumptuously with nothing to pay. The treaty had still to be ratified by the senate before its provisions could be carried out and the settlement made. This took about two years.

Figure 51. Farewell War-Dance of the Indians, August 18, 1835.

The money paid and the goods delivered, the Indians shook the dust off their feet and departed; the dust shaking being literal, for once, as they joined, just before starting, in a final "war-dance." For this strange scene, we fortunately have as witness Ex-Chief-Justice Caton, previously quoted herein. He estimates the dancers at eight hundred, that being all the braves that could be mustered, out of the five thousand members then present of the departing tribes. The date was August 18th, 1835. He says:

> They appreciated that it was their last on their native soil—that it was a sort of funeral ceremony of old associations and memories, and nothing was omitted to lend it all the grandeur and solemnity possible. They assembled at the Council House (North-east corner of Rush and Kinzie Streets). All were naked except a strip of cloth around their loins. Their bodies were covered with a great variety of brilliant paints. On their faces particularly they seemed to have exhausted their art of hideous decoration. Foreheads, cheeks and noses were covered with curved strips of red or vermillion, which were edged with black points, and gave the appearance of a horrid grin. The long, coarse black hair was gathered into

scalp locks on the tops of their heads and decorated with a profusion of hawks' and eagles' feathers; some strung together so as to reach nearly to the ground. They were principally armed with tomahawks and war clubs. They were led by what answered for a band of music, which created a discordant din of hideous noises, produced by beating on hollow vessels and striking clubs and sticks together. They advanced with a continuous dance. Their actual progress was quite slow. They proceeded up along the river on the North side, stopping in front of every house to perform some extra antics. They crossed the north branch on the old bridge, about Kinzie Street, and proceeded south to the bridge which stood where Lake Street bridge is now, nearly in front of, and in full view from the Sauganash Hotel ("Wigwam" lot, Lake and Market Streets). A number of young married people had rooms there. The parlor was in the second story pointing west, from the windows of which the best view of the dancers was to be had and these were filled with ladies.

The young lawyer, afterward Chief Justice, had come to the West in 1833, and less than a year before this had gone back to Oneida County, New York, and there married Miss Laura Sherrill. They were among the lookers-on from those upper windows, a crowd all interested, many agitated and some really frightened at the thought of the passions and memories that must be inflaming those savage breasts and that were making them the very picture of demoniac fury.

Although the din and clatter had been heard for some time, they did not come into view from this point of observation till they had proceeded so far West (on the North side) as to come on a line with the house. All the way to the South Branch bridge came the wild band, which was in front as they came upon the bridge, redoubling their blows, followed by the warriors who had now wrought themselves into a perfect fury.

The morning was very warm and the perspiration was pouring from them. Their countenances had assumed an expression of all the worst passions—fierce anger, terrible hate, dire revenge, remorseless cruelty— all were expressed in their terrible features. Their tomahawks and clubs were thrown and brandished in every direction, and with every step and every gesture they uttered the most frightful yells. The dance consisted of leaps and spasmodic steps, now forward, now back or sidewise, the whole body distorted into every imaginable position, most generally stooping forward with the head and face thrown up, the back arched down, first one foot thrown forward and withdrawn and the other similarly thrust out, frequently squatting quite to the ground, and all with a movement almost as quick as lightning. The yells and screams they uttered were broken up and multiplied and rendered all the more hideous by a rapid clapping of the mouth with the palm of the hand. When the head of the column reached the hotel, while they looked up at the windows at the "Chemo-ko-man squaws," it seemed as if we had a picture of hell itself before us, and a carnival of the damned spirits there confined. They paused in their progress, for extra exploits, in front of John T. Semple's house, near the northwest corner of Lake and Franklin Streets, and then again in front of the Tremont, on the northwest corner of Take and Dearborn Streets, where the appearance of ladies again in the window again inspired them with new life and energy. Thence they proceeded down to Fort Dearborn, where we will take a final leave of my old friends, with more good wishes for their final welfare than I really dare hope will be realized.

The Indians were conveyed to the lands selected for them, (and accepted by a deputation sent by them in advance of the treaty) in Clay County, Missouri, opposite Fort Leavenworth, Kansas. The Missourians were hostile to their new, strange neighbors, and two years later they were again moved, this time to a reservation in Iowa, near Council Bluffs. Once more the fate of the poor waif, "Move on, move on," was theirs, and then they halted in Kansas for many years. Their present condition has been already sketched.

Judge Caton is an ardent, devoted friend of the Indians. He knew many of them personally, they having been his faithful companions—by night and day, in summer and winter—in hunting, which was the passion of his early years. Yet here, we observe, he says sadly, that his wishes for their welfare go beyond any confident hope he can feel.

APPENDIX K.

THE BRONZE MEMORIAL GROUP

History places the scene of the Massacre adjacent to the shore of Lake Michigan, between the present 16th and 20th Streets. The Memorial Group, now (1893) newly erected, stands at the eastern extremity of 18th Street, overlooking the lake (nothing intervening save the right of way of the Illinois Central Railway); and is therefore in the midst of the battle-field.

I think it well here to put in evidence unanswerable testimony as to the identity of the spot selected for the group with the place where the short and fatal struggle took place. Regarding it, Munsell's history observes:

> The attack, the charge, the subsequent advance, etc., seem all to point to about the spot where is now Eighteenth Street; and to the Massacre tree, a tall cottonwood, still standing when these lines are penned (1892), though dead since about five years ago.
>
> For conclusive evidence of the identity of the tree and its trustworthiness as marking the battle-field, see certificates of old citizens given on page 31, Vol. I, Andreas' History of Chicago.

The letters quoted by Captain Andreas are all from persons not only well-informed, but also of the highest social character and standing. They are as follows:

LETTER FROM MRS. HENRY W. KING

151 Rush Street, Chicago,
January 25, 1884.
A. T. Andreas, Esq.

Dear sir:—I am very happy to tell you what I know about the tree in question, for I am anxious that its value as a relic should be appreciated by Chicago people, especially since the fire has obliterated nearly every other object connected with our early history. Shortly before the death of my friend Mrs. John K. Kinzie, I called upon her and asked her to drive with me through the city and point out the various locations and points of interest that she knew were connected with the "early day" of Chicago. She said there were very few objects remaining, but localities she would be happy to show me.

She appointed a day, but was not well enough to keep her appointment; went East soon after for her health and died within a few weeks. However, at this interview I mention, she said that to her the most interesting object in our city was the old Cottonwood tree that stands on Eighteenth Street, between Prairie Avenue and the lake. She remarked that it, with its fellows, were saplings at the time of the Indian Massacre, and that they marked the spot of that fearful occurrence; though she was not sure but that the smaller one had either died or been cut down. I expressed surprise at the location, imagining that the massacre occurred further south, among the small sand-hills that we early settlers remember in the vicinity of Hyde Park. I remember that her answer to this was:

"My child, you must understand that in 1812 there was no Chicago, and the distance between the old fort and Eighteenth Street was enormous." Said she: "My husband and his family always bore in mind the location of that massacre, and marked it by the Cottonwood trees, which, strange to say, have stood unharmed in the middle of the street to this day."

The above facts I communicated to the Historical Society soon after Mrs. Kinzie's death, and believe through them was the means of preventing the cutting down of the old tree, which the citizens of the South Side had voted to be a nuisance. I sincerely hope something may be done to fence in and preserve so valuable a relic and reminder of one of the most sad and interesting events in the life of Chicago.

Believe me, sir, yours most respectfully,

Mrs. Henry W. King.

LETTER FROM HON. ISAAC N. ARNOLD

Chicago, January 25, 1884.

Captain A. T. Andreas.

Dear sir:—I have your note of this morning, asking me to state what I know relating to the massacre at Chicago in 1812. I came to Chicago in October, 1836; the Fort Dearborn reservation then, and for several years afterward, belonged to the government, and there were but a few scattering houses from Fort Dearborn south to [the present location of] the University, and between Michigan Avenue and the beach of Lake Michigan. The sand-hills near the shore were still standing. The family of John H. Kinzie was then the most prominent in Chicago, and the best acquainted with its early history. From this family and other early settlers, and by Mr. and Mrs. Kinzie, I was told where the attack on the soldiers by the Indians was made. There were then growing some cottonwood trees near which I was told the massacre occurred. One of those trees is still standing in the street leading from Michigan Avenue to the lake and not very far from the track of the Illinois Central Railway. This tree was pointed out to me by both Mr. and Mrs Kinzie, as near the place where the attack began. As the fight continued, the combatants moved south and went over considerable space. Mrs. John H. Kinzie was a person of clear and retentive memory and of great intelligence. She wrote a full and graphic history of the massacre, obtaining her facts, in part, from eye-witnesses, and I have no' doubts of her accuracy.

Very respectfully yours,

Isaac N. Arnold.

Letter from A. J. Galloway

Chicago, February 8, 1884.
Captain A. T. Andreas.

My dear sir:—At your request I will state my recollections concerning the cottonwood tree in the east end of Eighteenth Street. When I removed from Eldredge Court to the present 1808 Prairie Avenue, in 1858, the tree was in apparent good condition, though showing all the marks of advanced age. The large lower branches (since cutoff), after mounting upward for a time, curved gracefully downward, so that a man riding under them could have readily touched their extremities with his whip at a distance of twenty or twenty-five feet from the body. From an intimate knowledge of the growth of trees, I have no doubt but its sapling life long ante-dated the time of the massacre of the Fort Dearborn garrison. I will venture the opinion that if it were cut down and the stump subjected to a careful examination, it would be found that the last two inches of its growth cover a period of fifty years at least.

Yours truly,
A. J. Galloway.

To these highly convincing letters. Captain Andreas adds verbal testimony as follows:

Charles Harpell, an old citizen, now living on the North Side, says that as far back as he can remember this locality was known as "the Indian battle-ground;" that years ago, when a boy, he with others used to play there (the place, from its very associations, having the strongest attractions) and hunt in the sand for beads and other little trinkets, which they were wont to find in abundance. Mr. Harpell relates, also, that he, while playing there one day, found an old single-barreled brass pistol, which he kept for many years.

Mrs. Mary Clark Williams, whose father, H. B. Clark, purchased in 1833, the land on which the tree now stands, says that nearly fifty years ago she played under the old cottonwood, and that it was then a large and thrifty tree. In 1840 an old Indian told her that the massacre occurred on that spot.

On the same branch of the subject, and in absolute conformation of the Clark testimony, see the following letter, later than the other, which I am glad to be able to give as "the conclusion of the matter."

Aspen, Colorado, March 15, 1890.

Editor of the *Tribune:*

I notice your interesting article on the subject of the Chicago Massacre of 1812. I was born on what is now Michigan Avenue (then a farm) and within 1,200 feet of this awful affair. Your article is in the main correct, though not exactly so as regards the tree at the foot of Eighteenth Street. This was one of a grove, consisting of perhaps fifty to seventy-five large cotton-woods, extending from a little north of Sixteenth to a little south of Eighteenth Street. Almost in the center of this grove—I think the exact location would be two hundred and fifty to three hundred feet north of Eighteenth Street, on the east end of Wirt Dexter's lot—stood a "clump" of eight or nine trees....

The sand-hills extended from about where the Illinois Central round-house now is south to about Twenty-Fifth Street. They were covered with low cedar trees, ground pine, and sand cherry bushes, together with a perfect mat of sand prickers, to which the soles of our feet often gave testimony when in swimming. The old cemetery, where many of the old settlers were buried, was located near Twenty-Second Street and Calumet Avenue. I think the McAvoy brewery stands about the centre of it.

I sincerely hope something will be done to commemorate this awful affair and perpetuate the memory of our ancestors, who fought the Indians, the fleas and the ague to make so grand and beautiful a city as Chicago.

Robert G. Clarke.

So much for the place selected for the bronze group, now for the work itself.

Carl Rohl-Smith, a Danish sculptor who had already won distinction in Europe and in America, and who came to Chicago under the strong attraction which the preparation of the World's Columbian Exposition offered for all artists, won notice and praise by his statue of Franklin, cast for the entrance of the Electrical building. This work pleased those interested highly, and the sculptor was invited to prepare the model for a group to commemorate the Fort Dearborn Massacre of 1812. Mr. Rohl-Smith, by the help of his accomplished wife, made a study of the historical facts connected with the event, and naturally concluded that Black Partridge saving the life of Mrs. Helm was the portion of the sad story which presented the most picturesque, dramatic and artistic features for reproduction. To this he added the killing of Surgeon VanVoorhees, which Mrs. Helm details almost in the same breath with the story of her own experience. The study, when completed in clay, won the approval of all observers (this acceptance being fortified by the warm admiration the group elicited from the best art-critics to whom it was submitted), and orders were at once given for the work; to be in bronze and of heroic proportions; the figure group to be nine feet high, set on a granite pedestal ten feet high.

Mr. Rohl-Smith set himself to work with the utmost diligence. Fortune favored him; for there happened to be just then some Indians of the must untamed sort at Fort Sheridan (only a few miles away), in charge of the garrison as prisoners of war, they having been captured in the Pine Ridge disturbance whereof the affair of Wounded Knee creek was the chief event. By General Miles's permission, Mr. Rohl-Smith was allowed to select two of these red-men to stand as models for the principal savage figures of the group. The two best adapted were "Kicking Bear" and "Short Bull." Concerning them Mr. Rohl-Smith says:

> Kicking Bear is the best specimen of physical manhood I have ever critically examined. He is a wonderful man and seems to enjoy the novelty of posing, besides evidently having a clear understanding of the use to which his figure will be put. The assailant of Mrs. Helm, the one with the uplifted tomahawk [Short Bull] fills the historical idea that the assailant was a "young" Indian, naturally one who would not be as fully developed as the vigorous, manly chief, Black Partridge. The presence of these Indians has been of great value to me in producing the figures. I have been enabled to bring out some of their characteristics not otherwise possible.

The savages were accompanied by an interpreter, and the newspapers of the day gave some amusing accounts of their demeanor in the studio; their mixture of docility and self-assertion, etc. It chanced that the real dispositions of the two principal models were the reverse of their assumed characters; and Kicking Bear (who, when wearing his native dress and war-paint, carried a string of six scalps as part of his outfit), was much amused at the fact that he was assigned the more humane part. "Me, good Injun!" he cried; "him bad Injun!" And he laughed loudly at the jest.

The four faces of the granite pedestal bear appropriate bas-reliefs cast in bronze. The front (south-west) shows the fight itself; the opposite side represents the train—troops, wagons, etc.—leaving the fort; one end gives the scene when Black Partridge delivered up his medal to Captain Heald, and the opposite end the death of the heroic Wells.

The various scenes bear descriptive inscriptions; and on the North-West face is the dedication, as follows:

Presented May, 1893, to the Chicago Historical Society, in Trust for the City of Chicago and for Posterity.

The group stands on the scene of the fight, just one hundred and twenty feet east of the "Massacre tree" spoken of in chapter 7, and earlier in this appendix. Its position is admirable in the artistic point of view as well as in the historical, for it occupies the eastern extremity of Eighteenth Street and the northern of Calumet Avenue; separated from Lake Michigan only by the right of way of the Illinois Central railway. The hillocks which shielded the Indians in making their attack have been leveled down, but their sandy base forms an admirable foundation for the massive pedestal, which may well keep its place, unmoved, for a thousand years.

INDEX

A

Abbott, Dr. Lucius, 29
agency house, 50, 61, 188
Ah-mah-qua-zah-quah, 17, 166
Allen, Colonel, 91
Andrews, Presley, 132
Artaguiette, 106
Atwater, Major, 96

B

Bates, Eli, 109
Battles, Joe, 44
Baxley, Virginia, 189
Beaubien, Alex, 103
Bisson, Mrs., 26, 27
Black Bird, 21
Black Hawk, 13, 194
Black Partridge, x, 10, 11, 25, 26, 27, 72, 73, 86, 87, 212, 213
Black Partridge Medal, x, 73
Blanchard, Rufus, 145
Block-House, x, 102, 107, 109
Block-House Tablet, x, 107, 109

Bowen, Joseph, 100
British and Indians, 28, 60, 63
Burman, 128
Burns, John, 54, 76
Burns, Robert, 115
Butterfield, Justin, 130

C

Cahokia, 118, 181
Caldwell, Billy (Sauganash), xi, 27, 28, 196, 199, 205
Callis, Mrs., 29
Calumet Club, x, xi, 17, 104, 108, 192, 195
Calumet Lake, 38
Chandonnais, 19, 23, 24, 79, 83, 84
Charlotte, Queen, 96
Chicago, v, vii, viii, ix, x, 5, 6, 11, 14, 16, 19, 25, 26, 28, 29, 31, 33, 36, 37, 38, 40, 42, 43, 45, 48, 49, 50, 52, 54, 56, 60, 61, 66, 72, 79, 84, 86, 87, 89, 96, 97, 100, 101, 102, 103, 108, 109, 110, 113, 114, 116, 117, 118, 119, 120, 121, 122, 125, 127, 129, 130, 131, 136, 137, 138, 139, 141, 144, 145, 146, 147, 148, 149, 150, 151, 154, 157, 159, 160, 168, 173, 174,

176, 179, 181, 184, 186, 188, 189, 190, 191, 193, 194, 195, 199, 203, 207, 208, 209, 210, 211, 214
Clark, H. B., 210
Clark, John K., xi, 146
Clarke, Robert G., 211
Cleaver, Charles, 103
Clybourn, Archibald, xi, 147, 148
Clybourn, Jonas, 147
Cobweb Castle, 29, 188, 189
Confute Indians, 99, 100
Cooper, John, 132, 195
Corbin, James, 100, 102, 133
Corbin, Phelim, 2, 100, 102
Corbin, Sukey, 29
Custer slaughter, 14

D

Debou (Frenchman), 26, 40, 55, 56, 82, 104, 175, 181, 189, 190
defence, 73, 98, 124, 141, 184
Durantaye, 140
Dyer, Dyson, 100, 102, 133

E

Eastman, Lieut. J. L., 96
Edson, Nathan, 100, 102, 133
Epeconier, 16, 17
evacuation of Fort Dearborn, 71

F

Fergus, Robert, 186
Fergus, Scott, 186
Ferson, Julia, 136, 139
Forsyth, Robert, 144, 149, 157
Forsyth, Thomas, 83, 144, 150, 154
Forsyth, William, 144

Fort Chartres, 106, 114
Fort Dearborn, v, vii, viii, ix, 2, 36, 42, 45, 47, 48, 49, 51, 52, 53, 63, 64, 74, 81, 96, 101, 106, 109, 123, 124, 125, 126, 127, 129, 135, 136, 138, 140, 141, 149, 150, 154, 157, 171, 180, 181, 193, 195, 206, 209, 210, 212
Fort George, Canada, 84
Fort Maiden, Canada, 91
Fort Meigs, Canada, 91
François, 83, 120
Freer, Dr. Otto, 186
French Period, 36
Fury, John, 133

G

Galloway, A. J., 210
Glamorgan, 118, 120
Gordon, Mrs. Nellie Kinzie, 160
Great Fire, viii, xi, 129

H

Haliburton, Mrs., 144
Hall, Benjamin, 147
Hall, David, 148
Hall, Eugene, 109
Hallam, Rev. Mr., 190
hardscrabble, 53, 61, 87
Harpell, Charles, 210
Harrison, W. H., 168, 171
Hays, Sergeant, 88
Heald, Captain Nathan, 14, 18, 51, 125, 131, 132, 177
Heald, Hon. Darius, viii, 5, 12, 19, 65, 166, 173
Heald, Rebekah, 12, 173
Helm, Lieut. Linai T., 101
Helm, Margaret, 3, 7
Hennepin, 114

Henry, Patrick, 116
Hispaniola, 118
Historical Society, viii, xi, 11, 26, 29, 109, 118, 120, 154, 179, 180, 186, 191, 209, 214
Hoyt, William M., viii, 109
Hubbard, G. S., 184

I

Indian Group, 109
Indians, xi, 3, 5, 6, 7, 9, 13, 14, 15, 16, 18, 19, 20, 21, 22, 25, 26, 27, 28, 30, 36, 37, 38, 41, 43, 45, 48, 52, 54, 56, 60, 63, 64, 65, 67, 68, 70, 71, 72, 74, 75, 79, 80, 81, 82, 86, 88, 91, 96, 97, 98, 99, 100, 101, 103, 104, 105, 106, 113, 116, 117, 119, 120, 124, 125, 129, 130, 136, 140, 149, 150, 153, 154, 158, 159, 160, 166, 167, 169, 170, 171, 173, 174, 175, 176, 180, 181, 182, 193, 195, 196, 199, 203, 204, 206, 209, 211, 212, 214

J

Jackson, Samuel, 189
Jefferson, President, 40, 124
Johnston, John, 168
Jones, Fernando, 103, 104, 187, 188, 189, 190
Jordan, Walter, 98, 100
Jouett, Charles, ix, 43, 44

K

Kaskaskia, 118, 120, 124
Keamble, 128
Kee-po-tah, 23, 25, 83, 84, 93
Kicking Bear, 212, 213
King, Mrs. Henry W., 208, 209

Kingston, John T., 118
Kinzie family, xi, 5, 7, 23, 98, 102, 141, 143, 152
Kinzie House, x, 2, 45, 76, 93, 156, 186, 189
Kinzie, Ellen Marion, 160
Kinzie, John, v, 3, 6, 11, 26, 42, 43, 50, 51, 54, 60, 64, 75, 76, 85, 89, 90, 118, 138, 142, 143, 144, 146, 148, 149, 150, 154, 155, 160, 180, 183, 184, 188, 189
Kinzie, John Harris, xi, 43, 141, 149, 152, 155, 161, 162
Kinzie, Mrs. John, 5, 23, 54, 102, 149
Kinzie, Robert Allen, xi, 156
Knowles, Joseph, 100

L

Laframboise, Pierre, 189
Lalime, John, 53, 151, 179, 180, 181, 186, 189, 190
Latrobe, John Joseph, 203
Law, John, 114, 118
Lawe, Judge John, 48
Le Mai, 39, 42, 118, 140, 149, 155
Leclerc, Peresh, 11, 20, 21
Liber Scriptorum, 121
Lincoln, Hon. Robert, 51, 124
Little Turtle (Me-che-kan-nah-quah), ix, 13, 17, 37, 38, 166, 167, 168, 169, 171
Locker, Frederick, 133
Logan, Hugh, 101, 102, 133
Lynch, Michael, 133

M

Mackinaw, 50, 63, 79, 80, 85, 89, 114, 116, 153
Macomb, Mr., 93
Mad Anthony, 28, 37, 168
Main Poc, 182

Marquette, 36, 54, 87, 114
Massacre, v, vii, x, xi, 1, 14, 61, 95, 172, 178, 207, 208, 211, 212, 214
Massacre tree, x, xi, 95, 178, 207, 214
McCagg, Ezra, 187
McCoy, Isaac, 45
McKenzie, Elizabeth, 145
McKenzie, Isaac, 147
McKenzie, John, 144
McKenzie, Margaret, 150, 153
McKillip, Margaret, 6, 149
McPherson, Hugh, 132
Me-che-kan-nah-quah, ix, 17, 37, 38, 166
Miami Indians, 6, 71, 98
Militia-men, 125
Miller, Samuel, 148
Mills, Elias, 100
Mirandeau, Victoire, 184
Mott, August, 101, 102, 133
Mound City (gun-boat), 92, 161

N

Napoleonic years, 45
Nau-non-gee, 60, 88
Neads, John, 101, 102, 134
Nee-scot-nee-meg, 26
Nelson, 101
Noble, Mark, 159
Noke-no-qua, Miss, 182

O

O'Strander, Philip, 132
Ottawas, 60, 105, 144, 154
Ouillemette, 2, 40, 76

P

Parc-aux-vaches, 5, 98, 154

Patterson, Mr., 91
Pee-so-tum, 11, 22, 23
Pe-me-zah-quah, 166
Peterson, 128, 134
Pope, Nathaniel, 166
Pottowatomies, x, 6, 8, 25, 28, 40, 45, 55, 60, 70, 83, 85, 105, 119, 120, 144, 154
Put-in-bay, 89

R

Robinson, Chief, 79
Rohl-Smith, Carl, 11, 211
Round Head, 200
Rumsey, Julian, 199
Ryerson, Martin, 109

S

sand-dunes, 7
Senat, Jesuit, 106
Shaubena, x, 119
Shaw-nee-aw-kee (Silver-smith), 51, 91, 144
Short Bull, 212
Smith, John, 132, 134
St. Ange, 106
St. Cosme, 114
St. James' Church, 190
St. Joseph's, 5, 6, 41, 42, 80, 83, 84, 85, 139, 147, 149, 154

T

Tanner, Dr. H. B., 48
Taylor, Augustus, 162
Tecumseh, x, 13, 28, 88, 200, 201
Thompson, Lieut., 189
Tonti, 37, 114
To-pee-nee-be, 6, 82, 84

Toussaint L'Ouverture, 118
Tree, Lambert, 109

V

Van Home, James, 102, 134
Vinsenne, 106

W

Wabash Indians, 25, 82
Wabash River, 25, 167
Wa-bin-she-way, 29
Waggoner, Anthony L., 134
Wah-bee-nee-mah, 11, 12
Walk-in-the-water, 200
Wa-nan-ga-peth, 17, 166
War-dance, xi, 203, 204
Washington, President, 168
Waubansa stone, xi, 129, 130
Wau-ban-see, 22, 27
Wau-Bun, x, xi, 3, 4, 5, 6, 10, 12, 20, 23, 26, 28, 30, 43, 54, 60, 62, 63, 64, 68, 70, 71, 72, 80, 82, 84, 85, 86, 93, 97, 117, 144, 150, 151, 158, 160, 181, 185, 199
Webster, Daniel, 130
Weem-tee-gosh, 82

Wells Street, 119, 157
Wells, Rebekah, 3, 18, 51, 71, 165, 167, 173
Wells, Samuel, 18, 19, 51, 81, 166, 167, 173
Wells, William, x, 3, 6, 18, 38, 48, 71, 75, 165, 166, 167, 168, 169, 170, 171
Wentworth, John, viii, 135, 169, 183, 193
Whistler family, 135
Whistler, John, 40, 51, 135, 137, 139, 141, 150
Whistler, John Jr., 150
Whistler, William, ix, 40, 41, 42, 136, 139, 140, 141
White Elk, 29
White, Liberty, 53, 56
Williams, Mrs. Mary Clark, 210
Wilmette, 40
Winnebagoes, 56, 60, 70
Winnemeg, 22, 63
Wolcott, Alexander, 5, 154
Wolcott, Henry Clay, 166
Wolcott, James Madison, 17, 166, 171
Wolcott, William Wells, 166
Wood, Alonzo C., 190
Woodward, Augustus B., 29

Related Nova Publications

The American Revolution. Volume II

Author: John Fiske

Series: American History, Culture and Literature

Book Description: This 2 part history of the American Revolution was written right after the Civil War. The author's insight into not only what was happening in the United States but also to all that was occurring in Great Britain makes this book as relevant today as when it was first written.

Hardcover ISBN: 978-1-53615-026-1
Retail Price: $230

Naval Actions of the War of 1812

Author: James Barnes

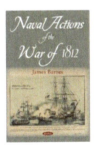

Series: American History, Culture and Literature

Book Description: *Naval Actions of the War of 1812* was previously published in 1896 to study the condition of affairs that led up to the declaration of the second war against Great Britain.

Softcover ISBN: 978-1-53614-626-4
Retail Price: $95

To see a complete list of Nova publications, please visit our website at www.novapublishers.com

Related Nova Publications

THE ARCHITECTURE OF COLONIAL AMERICA

AUTHORS: Harold Donaldson Eberlein and Mary H. Northend

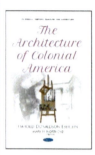

SERIES: American History, Culture and Literature

BOOK DESCRIPTION: *The Architecture of Colonial America* sets forth a brief history and an analysis of the architecture of Colonial America, in such a way that they may be of interest and value both to the general reader and to the architect.

HARDCOVER ISBN: 978-1-53615-878-6
RETAIL PRICE: $160

A BIOGRAPHY OF THE SIGNERS OF THE DECLARATION OF INDEPENDENCE, AND OF WASHINGTON AND PATRICK HENRY: WITH AN APPENDIX, CONTAINING THE CONSTITUTION OF THE UNITED STATES AND OTHER DOCUMENTS

AUTHOR: L. Carroll Judson

SERIES: American History, Culture and Literature

BOOK DESCRIPTION: *A Biography of the Signers of the Declaration of Independence* contains biographies of individuals who wisely conceived, nobly planned and boldly achieved the independence of these United States.

HARDCOVER ISBN: 978-1-53615-872-4
RETAIL PRICE: $230

To see a complete list of Nova publications, please visit our website at www.novapublishers.com